S. Hrg. 114–14

S. 438, the IRRIGATE Act

HEARING

BEFORE THE

COMMITTEE ON INDIAN AFFAIRS
UNITED STATES SENATE

ONE HUNDRED FOURTEENTH CONGRESS

FIRST SESSION

_____

MARCH 4, 2015

_____

Printed for the use of the Committee on Indian Affairs

U.S. GOVERNMENT PUBLISHING OFFICE

94–556 PDF   WASHINGTON : 2015

_____

For sale by the Superintendent of Documents, U.S. Government Publishing Office
Internet: bookstore.gpo.gov   Phone: toll free (866) 512–1800; DC area (202) 512–1800
Fax: (202) 512–2104   Mail: Stop IDCC, Washington, DC 20402–0001

CONTENTS

S. 438, the IRRIGATE Act

WEDNESDAY, MARCH 4, 2015

U.S. SENATE,
COMMITTEE ON INDIAN AFFAIRS,
Washington, DC.

The Committee met, pursuant to notice, at 2:30 p.m. in room 628, Dirksen Senate Office Building, Hon. John Barrasso, Chairman of the Committee, presiding.

OPENING STATEMENT OF HON. JOHN BARRASSO, U.S. SENATOR FROM WYOMING

The CHAIRMAN. Good afternoon. I call this hearing to order.

Today, the Committee will examine S. 438, the Irrigation Rehabilitation and Renovation for Indian Tribal Governments and Their Economies Act or the IRRIGATE Act.

Senator Tester and I introduced the IRRIGATE Act with bipartisan support, earlier this month. I want to thank him, along with Senator Daines, Senator Mike Enzi, Senator Orrin Hatch, and Senator Michael Bennet, for co-sponsoring this important piece of legislation.

I also want to welcome my friends, Harry LaBonde, Director, Wyoming Water Development Commission. Thank you very much for being here. I welcome Mitch Cottenoir, the Tribal Water Engineer of the Eastern Shoshone and Northern Arapaho Tribes in Wyoming. Mr. Cottenoir has testified before this Committee on irrigation issues in the past. Both witnesses are very familiar with the challenges facing irrigation projects.

In the late 1880s and early 1890s, the Department of Interior initiated irrigation projects across Indian reservations in the west. These irrigation projects were intended to be a central component for tribal economies. Construction of these projects ended sometime in the 1940s and many irrigation projects were never fully completed. In 2006, the Government Accountability Office found many of these projects were plagued by maintenance issues, structural deficiencies and insufficient funding for project operations.

In recent years, the Committee has held two hearings on Indian irrigation projects, a field hearing in Wyoming in 2011 and an oversight hearing in September 2014. Those hearings confirmed a serious backlog in deferred maintenance exists and continues to grow.

Many ranchers and farmers, both Indian and non-Indian, still depend on the Bureau of Indian Affairs to deliver water for their needs. While the Bureau has indicated the current backlog costs

(1)

exceed $567 million, some Indian tribes have estimated it may be even higher than that, much higher.

Today, the Indian Irrigation Program is responsible for the oversight and administration of these projects that deliver water to over 25,000 users. One of these projects is on the Wind River Reservation in my home State of Wyoming.

The photos before the dais are taken from various parts of the Wind River Irrigation Project. In the photos you see before you, there is a comparison of structures on the reservation. The left photo represents the ancient deteriorating infrastructure still in use on the reservation. The other photo represents the dramatic improvement that has occurred in the few areas where these systems are rehabilitated and adequately maintained.

The next set of photos shows the basics of the irrigation system. On the left, you see the grating system put in place by the Bureau of Indian Affairs. You can also see the brush overgrown around the canal.

On the right, you see that modest rehabilitation efforts can transform these structures. In this case, the tribes contributed with the State for that rehabilitation.

This legislation would also facilitate more collaboration between the tribes and the States. Many other Indian irrigation projects are in the States of members who sit on this Committee, including Montana, Washington, Arizona, New Mexico and Idaho.

Careful management of the water in Indian communities is essential if we are to ensure a reliable supply for the future. The IRRIGATE Act would bring the Indian irrigation projects into the 21st century.

It would authorize $35 million each year beginning in fiscal year 2016 until fiscal year 2036 to begin addressing the deferred maintenance needs. The bill would also require a study on the operation of these projects. These projects continue to be a very important source of income and economic development for the surrounding communities.

The Federal Government's promises to Indian country to build and maintain these projects needs to be fulfilled. This bill is a start in the right direction.

Finally, I am disappointed that the Department of Interior did not submit their testimony until 11:15 a.m. this morning. I understand it was not necessarily the department delaying the testimony but rather the Office of Management and Budget.

Regardless, I hope we don't see this happen again. These delays only serve to diminish the productivity of these important hearings.

Vice Chairman Tester, would you like to make an opening statement?

STATEMENT OF HON. JON TESTER, U.S. SENATOR FROM MONTANA

Senator TESTER. I would and thank you, Mr. Chairman. I appreciate your holding this legislative hearing on the IRRIGATE Act.

I also want to thank Councilman Headdress for being here today and making the trip from Fort Peck. We send our thoughts and good wishes to Chairman Stefani as he continues to heal and recover back in Montana.

As Chairman Barrasso mentioned, irrigation systems are critical components on a number of reservations in Indian country. Unfortunately, what seems to be par for the course with a lot of tribal issues is we never have done a good job in ensuring the tribes have the resources they need to make these irrigation systems successful.

This bill is a step in the right direction as it provides the mechanism to fund deferred maintenance on these irrigation projects that have built up over decades. This bill would fund maintenance for 17 of the biggest irrigation projects across Indian country.

That is why I have joined the Chairman in sponsoring this bill. This bill was first included as a part of the authorized Rural Water Projects Completion Act in the last Congress. That bill had three components, all of which benefited Indian country.

In addition to irrigation provisions, that legislation would have finally provided funds to complete construction of six authorized rural water projects. Some of these projects are located on or near reservations but like irrigation systems, these projects benefit both Indian and non-Indian stakeholders throughout their service areas.

The Rural Water Projects bill would have also saved funding to pay for future tribal water settlements across the country. In each Congress, we are faced with a number of tribal water settlements that must be authorized. Instead of scrambling to find funds for each specific settlement, the Rural Water Projects bill would have created a dedicated funding stream similar to what has worked well in the past.

Several of the recently enacted tribal water rights settlements have actually included rehabilitating irrigation systems as well. In my mind, it really makes sense to consider these water issues in a more comprehensive manner.

I've also received letters from a number of tribes that support a larger package and who are interested in long term planning and funding for rural water projects and water settlements. I couldn't agree more.

We cannot continue to authorize water settlements and water projects without a plan to fund them. Accordingly, I expect to reintroduce the Rural Water Projects bill in the next few weeks. I look forward to working with my colleagues on this Committee and others to address the broader needs of Indian country.

For today, I am happy to hear from our witnesses about the importance of Indian irrigation systems in their communities and how we can work to improve those systems and address tribal water issues across the board.

With that, Mr. Chairman, I appreciate your holding the hearing. Thank you.

The CHAIRMAN. Thank you, Mr. Vice Chairman.

Senator Daines?

STATEMENT OF HON. STEVE DAINES, U.S. SENATOR FROM MONTANA

Senator DAINES. I want to give a warm welcome to Councilman Headdress. Welcome to Washington. You brought some of that Montana snow to the wrong place. We are going to send it back home, I think.

Thinking about your reservation, it is the size of Delaware, 2 million acres, 2,000 square miles. With a Vice President who comes from Delaware, we have a councilman here who has a reservation that is nearly the size of Delaware. It kind of helps us understand the scope required in these water projects and the importance of them.

I offer you a warm welcome from both Senator Tester and myself to Washington.

The CHAIRMAN. Thank you, Senator Daines.

We would now like to hear the testimony from our witnesses. Please try to keep your comments within five minutes.

We will start with the Honorable Kevin Washburn, Assistant Secretary, Indian Affairs, Department of the Interior.

STATEMENT OF HON. KEVIN WASHBURN, ASSISTANT SECRETARY—INDIAN AFFAIRS, DEPARTMENT OF THE INTERIOR

Mr. WASHBURN. Thank you, Chairman, Vice Chairman and Senator.

We are very happy to be here. I want to personally apologize about the lateness of our testimony. That is all on me. It is not OMB's fault. We have had a lot of hearings lately. In fact, the Secretary was testifying this morning at the Senator Appropriations Committee. It is hard for us to turn around testimony on time, we have so many hearings.

I will take ownership of that and again, I apologize because I know your staff needs time to prepare and you need time to prepare.

Thank you for your leadership on this issue. You and the Vice Chairman have had a laser-like focus on the importance of irrigation projects. I want to commend you for that. This issue would not be getting the attention it does if you hadn't kept it as focused.

In the interest of time, I am largely going to stand on my written testimony but I want to raise two modest pieces of good news for you before I stop.

First of all, I want to talk a little bit about the Land Buy Back Program. One piece of good news is the *Cobell* settlement which was negotiated by the Secretary of the Interior and the President and enacted by this Congress, this Committee had a big role in that, has made some forward progress.

One of our problems with irrigation systems is we need to assess the owners of interest in agricultural land, the trust land. Many of those are in fractionated ownership and we often don't bill the people that have tiny little interests. We are now consolidating those interests and that will produce more accessible land and ultimately produce better recoveries, more recovery of the cost of irrigation projects. That is one piece of good news.

The other piece of good news is the President's proposed budget which has a $1.5 million increase for irrigation O&M recommended to Congress. That is a roughly 12 or 13 percent increase over what we have in the current fiscal year.

The President has exercised some leadership. I realize it is modest leadership in this regard because we have a lot of priorities, but

I do want you to know we are trying to fund irrigation projects better.

I thank you again for your leadership. I think I will stop there and take your questions whenever you are ready.

[The prepared statement of Mr. Washburn follows:]

PREPARED STATEMENT OF HON. KEVIN WASHBURN, ASSISTANT SECRETARY—INDIAN AFFAIRS, DEPARTMENT OF THE INTERIOR

Good afternoon Chairman Barrasso, Vice Chairman Tester, and members of the Committee. My name is Kevin Washburn and I am the Assistant Secretary for Indian Affairs at the Department of the Interior (Department). Thank you for inviting the Department to provide testimony on S. 438, the Irrigation Rehabilitation and Renovation for Indian Tribal Governments and Their Economies Act, a bill to provide for the repair, replacement, and maintenance of certain Indian irrigation projects. We appreciate the Committee's continued leadership on the daunting challenge the Department faces on addressing the deferred maintenance at the 17 Bureau of Indian Affairs' (BIA) Irrigation projects.

Larry Roberts, Principal Deputy Assistant Secretary for Indian Affairs, for the Department, testified before this Committee last September and provided an overview of the Irrigation Projects in Indian Country, along with the BIA's Irrigation Program's accomplishments, Irrigation project condition assessments, and the deferred maintenance estimates for our 17 BIA Irrigation Projects. S. 438 seeks to address the deferred maintenance for the BIA's Irrigation Projects by identifying the eligible projects, establishing a priority for allocating $35 million per year to our BIA Irrigation projects for twenty-two years to carry out the maintenance, repair and replacement activities at the irrigation projects. S. 438 also provides for establishing programmatic goals and conducting a study aimed at improving program and project management, and performance of BIA irrigation projects with a report to be delivered to Congress within 2 years. The Department supports the goals of working with tribes to address the maintenance of irrigation projects, and we look forward to working with you to address the best means of doing so given current budget constraints and the ability of irrigation projects to financially sustain themselves in the long run.

Background

The Federal Government has been involved with Indian irrigation since the Colorado River Indian Irrigation Project was authorized in 1867. In the early 1900s, Congress began authorizing funding for the construction of numerous Indian irrigation projects in the western United States. At that time, the Indian Irrigation Service led construction and early administration of the projects. In the late 1930's and through the 1940s, as construction activities wrapped up on most projects, the Indian Irrigation Service ceased to exist and operation and maintenance (O&M) was transferred to the BIA, where it continues today. Many of these programs began at a time when Federal policies were far different. These irrigation projects remain very important today to the communities they serve. The BIA irrigation program is responsible for oversight and administration of fifteen revenue-generating Indian irrigation projects that provide service and water delivery to over 25,000 customers and 750,000 acres of land in Indian Country. The asset inventory and program responsibilities also include BIA-owned facilities at non-revenue generating irrigation projects, including the Navajo Indian Irrigation Project in New Mexico and Pyramid Lake Irrigation Project in northern Nevada. At these facilities the BIA does not assess O&M charges to irrigators; those charges are instead paid through appropriations or other means.

S. 438

S. 438 would create an "Indian Irrigation Fund" (IIF) in the Department of the Treasury from the reclamation fund that was established in the Act of June 17, 1902 (32 Stat. 388, chapter 1093). The IIF would be funded at $35 million per year for 22 years for a total investment of $770 million. The legislation also caps the year to year spending at $35 million, but includes amounts of interest earned on investments from the IIF, if applicable, "to carry out maintenance, repair and replacement activities" for one or more of the eligible Indian irrigations projects identified in Sec. 202 of the S. 438.

Section 104 requires the Secretary of the Interior to invest portions of the IFF that in the judgment of the Secretary are not required to meet current withdrawals. We recommend that the U.S. Treasury be designated as the federal agency responsible for investing IFF assets. We need to consult with the Department of the Treasury in more detail about these provisions.

Section 201(b) of S. 438 describes funding "to carry out maintenance, repair and replacement activities. . . .". The term "maintenance" is used and further states "including any structures, facilities, equipment, or vehicles used in connection with the operation of those projects." We interpret this language as authorizing funding for the purchase of heavy equipment to address some deferred maintenance items, conduct routine and preventative maintenance activities, and also to purchase vehicles to support water delivery/operation activities. If this is the case we request adding the term "personnel" to the list of items in parenthesis in Section 201(b) in order to clarify that hiring personnel is allowable in supporting O&M of the eligible projects.

Section 202 of S. 438 defines the eligible projects for the IIF. The following is a list of the 17 Irrigation Projects that meet the criteria listed in Section 202.

- Blackfeet Indian Irrigation Project (MT)
- Colorado River Indian Irrigation Project (AZ/CA)
- Crow Indian Irrigation Project (MT)
- Duck Valley Indian Irrigation Project (NV)
- Flathead Indian Irrigation Project (MT)
- Fort Belknap Indian Irrigation Project (MT)
- Fort Hall Indian Irrigation Project (ID)
- Fort Peck Indian Irrigation Project (MT)
- Navajo Indian Irrigation Project (NM)
- Pine River Indian Irrigation Project (CO)
- Pyramid Lake Indian Irrigation Project (NV)
- San Carlos Indian Irrigation Project—Indian Works (AZ)
- San Carlos Indian Irrigation Project—Joint Works (AZ)
- Uintah Indian Irrigation Project (UT)
- Walker River Indian Irrigation Project (NV)
- Wapato Indian Irrigation Project (WA)
- Wind River Indian Irrigation Project (WY)

We recommend amending Section 202(2), as follows: "are managed and operated by the Bureau of Indian Affairs (including projects managed, operated and/or maintained under contracts or compacts pursuant to the Indian Self-Determination and Education Assistance Act (25 U.S.C. 450 et seq.) or other agreements with water users, water user groups and/or water user associations; and. . . ." This is to ensure that the irrigation projects with 638 Contracts or Memorandum of Agreements (MOAs) with water user groups for O&M are not excluded.

Section 203, which refers to "requirements and condition," includes the Commissioner of Reclamation. Section 2 also describes the Secretary of the Interior as acting through the Commissioner or Reclamation. We recommend amending these references since the Bureau of Reclamation (Reclamation) is not involved in the operation and maintenance of the 17 eligible irrigation projects, nor is Reclamation involved in the allocation of resources among funds created within the Treasury. In Section 203(2)(E), regarding the funding prioritization criteria/methodology, the BIA has been collecting Condition Assessment data that BIA has used over the past decade. The BIA is initiating irrigation project Modernization Studies, which will provide additional and very valuable decisionmaking information on how BIA would best rehabilitate the existing irrigation project infrastructure. We recommend adding language to Section 203 that allow the results of the Modernization Studies to be incorporated into the criteria/methodology used in the implementation of S. 438.

Section 205 requires Tribal Consultation and Water User Input. As this Committee is aware, Tribal consultation can be a lengthy process, and we understand our responsibility to consult with affected tribes and water users for these 17 irrigation projects and to provide adequate notice to make such consultation meaningful, usually 30 days. In order to facilitate the consultation required under this Section, we recommend the timeframe be changed from "60 days" to a "not later than 120 days."

Section 206 of S. 438 provides a foundation for establishing which projects to prioritize and takes into consideration a reduced priority for those projects that have received funding by an "act of Congress" in the previous 15 year period. According to Section 206(b), the following projects have received funding under an "Act of Congress that expressly identifies the Indian irrigation project or the Indian reservation of the project to address the deferred maintenance, repair, or replacement needs of the Indian irrigation project:

- Crow Indian Irrigation Project, Crow Tribe Water Rights Settlement Act of 2010, Public Law 111–291, signed into law on December 8th, 2010.
- Duck Valley Indian Irrigation Project, 2009 Omnibus Public Land Management Act (H.R. 146, 111th Congress).
- San Carlos Indian Irrigation Project—Indian Works, Arizona Water Settlements Act, 118 STAT. 3478 PUBLIC LAW 108–451–DEC. 10, 2004.
- Navajo Indian Irrigation Project, Public Law No. 87–483, 76 Stat. 96 (1962) (NIIP Act)—receives annual appropriations for construction and maintenance activities.

Section 206(b) provides the "Priority" as first based on an Indian irrigation project(s) serving more than one Indian tribe within "an Indian reservation." Based on this requirement the following irrigation project would receive funding priority under S. 438 over the first few years.

Priority List:

The only Irrigation Project that serves more than one Indian tribe within an Indian reservation is:

- Wind River Indian Irrigation Project (Northern Arapahoe Tribe, Eastern Shoshone Tribe, Wind River Reservation).

The priorities identified next according to Sec. 203 "programmatic goals" to fulfill S. 438, and "critical maintenance needs" include the following Projects not listed in order of priorities:

- Blackfeet Indian Irrigation Project
- Colorado River Indian Irrigation Project
- Flathead Indian Irrigation Project
- Fort Belknap Indian Irrigation Project
- Fort Hall Indian Irrigation Project
- Fort Peck Indian Irrigation Project
- Pine River Indian Irrigation Project
- Pyramid Lake Indian Irrigation Project
- San Carlos Indian Irrigation Project—Joint Works
- Uintah Indian Irrigation Project
- Walker River Indian Irrigation Project
- Wapato Indian Irrigation Project

Irrigation Projects that serve only 1 Indian tribe within an Indian reservation but have received funds in last 15 years (if S. 438 enacted this year):

- Crow Indian Irrigation Project (received Settlement funds)
- Duck Valley Indian Irrigation Project (received Settlement funds)
- San Carlos Indian Irrigation Project—Indian Works (received Settlement funds)
- Navajo Indian Irrigation Project (receives annual appropriations)

Last September, we testified before this Committee that the BIA operates its irrigation projects consistent with numerous laws, regulations and policy guidance and many projects have extensive and specific legislative histories. For example, specific statutory authorities require that BIA charge an assessment to both Indian and non-Indian customers for O&M costs. Most of the 15 revenue-generating projects receive little or no appropriated funds. Whenever possible and practical, BIA works to leverage cost-share opportunities with any other funding that is made available to tribes and water user organizations. Funding to maintain these systems must also compete for other pressing priorities in Indian Country.

Historically, BIA has not charged sufficient Operation, Maintenance & Rehabilitation (OM&R) rates to allow for adequate project maintenance and replacement. Over time, this has resulted in less maintenance accomplished and a steady increase in deferred maintenance. This contributed to critical reviews by the Office of Inspector General in the 1990's and the Government Accountability Office in 2006. The 2013 deferred maintenance estimate for BIA-owned irrigation facilities is approximately $600 million. Less clear is what should be the appropriate allocation of responsibility between the users and beneficiaries of these systems, particularly by non-tribal members, and the general taxpayer.

Over the past 9 years we have increased our O&M rates an average of 26 percent across all projects. We believe that rates are approaching levels to stem the growth of deferred maintenance, but the existing level of deferred maintenance is such that it may be difficult to address through increased O&M rates alone. To ensure the protection of the investments that would be provided by this Act, BIA will continue to evaluate the O&M rates assessed to irrigators while considering the local agricultural economies. The BIA irrigation projects are vital economic contributors to the local communities and regions where they are located. The BIA estimates that irrigated lands served by the 15 BIA revenue generating irrigation projects add $490M in revenue and supports almost 10,000 jobs. This Administration supports investments in vital economic contributors and supports the goals of the bill, and we look forward to working with you to address the best means of doing so given current budget constraints and the ability of irrigation projects to financially sustain themselves in the long run.

This concludes my prepared statement. I will be happy to answer any questions you may have.

The CHAIRMAN. Thank you very much, Secretary Washburn.

Next, we have Ms. Anne-Marie Fennell, Director, Natural Resources and Environment, U.S. Government Accountability Office, Washington, D.C.

STATEMENT OF ANNE–MARIE FENNELL, DIRECTOR, NATURAL RESOURCES AND ENVIRONMENT, U.S. GOVERNMENT ACCOUNTABILITY OFFICE

Ms. FENNELL. Chairman Barrasso, Vice Chairman Tester and members of the Committee, I am pleased to be here today to participate in your hearing on S. 438, a bill to provide for the repair, replacement and maintenance of certain Indian irrigation Projects.

In February 2006, we reported on 16 irrigation projects where water users were charged for project operations and maintenance by BIA. These projects, some of which date back to the late 1880s, include water storage facilities and delivery structures for agricultural purposes, particularly critical in light of water scarcity out west, my testimony today will summarize the findings of our February 2006 report, along with updates and the status of the three recommendations we made in the report. Specifically, I will discuss BIA's estimated deferred maintenance costs for the irrigation projects, shortcomings we identified in BIA's management of its projects and issues we identified that needed to be addressed to determine the long term direction of BIA's program.

In our 2006 report, we found that BIA had estimated the cost for deferred maintenance at the 16 irrigation projects at about $850 million for fiscal year 2005. To further refine its cost estimate, BIA planned to hire engineering and irrigation experts to periodically conduct thorough condition assessments to identify deferred maintenance needs and costs. The irrigation projects included in the agency's estimate have changed somewhat since our report. The most recent estimate for fiscal year 2014 was reported just under $570 million.

In our report, we found BIA's management of some of its irrigation projects had serious shortcomings that undermined effective decision-making about project operations and maintenance. Specifically, under BIA's organizational structure, in many cases, officials with authority to oversee project manager decision-making lacked the expertise needed to do so effectively. While the staff who had the expertise, lacked the necessary authority to oversee project manager decisions.

We also found BIA did not consistently provide information and opportunities for stakeholders to participate in setting project priorities. We made two recommendations to address these management shortcomings, which BIA subsequently implemented.

In our report, we found the long term direction of BIA's irrigation program depended on the resolution of several larger issues. Of most importance, BIA did not know to what extent its irrigation projects were capable of financially sustaining themselves which hindered the agency's ability to address longstanding concerns regarding inadequate funding.

BIA also did not have a plan for how it would obtain funding to fix the deferred maintenance items, a significant challenge in times of tight budgets.

Given that BIA must balance irrigation management with many other missions, we reported that it may be beneficial to consider whether others such as tribes or water users could better manage some of these projects.

We recommended in our 2006 report that BIA conduct studies to determine how much it would cost to financially sustain each project and the extent to which water users have the ability to pay these costs. We were later informed that while the department agreed on the value of these studies, it did not have sufficient funds to conduct them.

In conclusion, BIA irrigation projects continue to face hundreds of millions of dollars of deferred maintenance needs. Senate bill S. 438, if enacted, could help address these needs and potentially some of the other larger issues that we reported on by establishing an Indian Irrigation Fund.

Chairman Barrasso, Vice Chairman Tester and members of the Committee, this completes my prepared statement. I am happy to respond to questions.

[The prepared statement of Ms. Fennell follows:]

PREPARED STATEMENT OF ANNE-MARIE FENNELL, DIRECTOR, NATURAL RESOURCES AND ENVIRONMENT, U.S. GOVERNMENT ACCOUNTABILITY OFFICE

INDIAN IRRIGATION PROJECTS—DEFERRED MAINTENANCE AND FINANCIAL SUSTAINABILITY ISSUES REMAIN UNRESOLVED

WHY GAO DID THIS STUDY

Over 100 irrigation projects and systems can be found on Indian reservations primarily across the western United States. The scarcity of water in much of the western United States makes irrigation critical to agricultural activities. In February 2006, GAO reported on 16 irrigation projects where BIA charged water users for the projects' operation and maintenance (GAO–06–314). These projects, which were generally constructed in the late 1800s and early 1900s, included water storage facilities and delivery structures for agricultural purposes.

This testimony is based on GAO's February 2006 report and updated information on BIA's fiscal year 2014 estimate of deferred maintenance and actions BIA has taken to address GAO's three recommendations. The testimony focuses on (1) BIA's estimated deferred maintenance cost for its irrigation projects, (2) shortcomings that GAO identified in BIA's management of its irrigation projects, and (3) issues GAO identified that needed to be addressed to determine the long-term direction of BIA's irrigation program.

GAO is not making any new recommendations in this testimony.

WHAT GAO FOUND

The Department of the Interior's Bureau of Indian Affairs (BIA) estimated the cost for deferred maintenance for the 16 irrigation projects covered in GAO's February 2006 report at about $850 million for fiscal year 2005. To further refine the estimate, BIA planned to hire engineering and irrigation experts to conduct thorough condition assessments of the irrigation projects to correctly identify deferred maintenance needs and costs. While the irrigation projects included in the estimate have changed somewhat in the 9 years since GAO's report, BIA's fiscal year 2014 cost estimate for deferred maintenance for its irrigation projects is about $570 million.

In its February 2006 report, GAO found BIA's management of some of its irrigation projects had serious shortcomings that undermined effective decisionmaking about project operations and maintenance. First, under BIA's organizational structure, officials with the authority to oversee irrigation project managers generally lacked the technical expertise needed to do so effectively, while the staff that had the expertise lacked the necessary authority to oversee project managers' decisionmaking. Second, BIA had not consistently provided project stakeholders, such as water users, with the necessary information or opportunities to participate in project decisionmaking, contrary to federal regulations that required BIA to consult with project stakeholders in setting project priorities. BIA has implemented GAO's two recommendations related to these management shortcomings.

In its February 2006 report, GAO found that the long-term direction of BIA's irrigation program depended on the resolution of several larger issues.

- Financial sustainability. BIA did not know to what extent its irrigation projects were capable of financially sustaining themselves, hindering its ability to address long-standing concerns regarding inadequate funding.
- Funding for deferred maintenance. BIA did not have a plan for how to obtain funding to fix deferred maintenance items—a significant challenge in times of tight budgets and competing priorities.
- Alternative project managers. Given BIA's many responsibilities in support of Indian communities, it might be more appropriate for other entities, such as tribes or water users, to manage some or all of the irrigation projects.

To obtain information on the long-term financial sustainability of each of the projects, GAO recommended that BIA conduct studies to determine how much it would cost to financially sustain each project and the extent to which water users on each project have the ability to pay these costs. Subsequently, in June 2008, the Department of the Interior stated in a memorandum that it did not have sufficient funding to perform these studies—and did not expect to have such funding in the foreseeable future. Since GAO's February 2006 report, BIA irrigation projects continue to face hundreds of millions of dollars of deferred maintenance needs, and financial sustainability issues also remain unresolved.

Chairman Barrasso, Vice Chairman Tester, and Members of the Committee:

I am pleased to be here today to participate in your hearing on S. 438—a bill to provide for the repair, replacement, and maintenance of certain Indian irrigation projects. There are over 100 irrigation projects and systems on Indian reservations primarily across the western United States. As you know, the scarcity of water in much of the western United States makes irrigation critical to the continued success of agricultural activities. In February 2006, we reported on 16 Indian irrigation projects where water users were charged for project operations and maintenance by the Department of the Interior's (Interior) Bureau of Indian Affairs (BIA), which is responsible for providing social and economic services to Indians as well as managing land and natural resources held in trust by the United States for Indians.[1]

Generally initiated in the late 1800s and early 1900s by Interior as part of the Federal Government's Indian assimilation policy, BIA's irrigation program was designed to foster agricultural opportunities and provide economic benefits to Indian communities. The 16 irrigation projects include water storage facilities and delivery structures for agricultural purposes. Over time, non-Indians began buying or leasing the land served by the projects for agricultural purposes, and project stakeholders evolved from Indian water users and the tribes within the reservations to include non-Indian water users as well. Many of the water users today are non-Indian.

Reports by Interior's Inspector General on BIA's irrigation projects have documented that the annual operations and maintenance fees BIA has charged water users have historically been set too low to cover the full cost of running the projects.[2] In addition, problems have been reported with collecting the fees that have been assessed. Because of insufficient funding, project maintenance has been consistently postponed, resulting in an extensive and costly list of deferred mainte-

---

[1] GAO, *Indian Irrigation Projects: Numerous Issues Need to Be Addressed to Improve Project Management and Financial Sustainability*, GAO–06–314 (Washington, D.C.: Feb. 24, 2006).

[2] Department of the Interior, Office of the Inspector General, *Indian Irrigation Projects, Bureau of Indian Affairs*, 96–I–641 (Washington D.C.: March 1996); Department of the Interior, Office of the Inspector General, *Operations and Maintenance Assessments of Indian Irrigation Projects, Bureau of Indian Affairs*, W–1A–BIA–12–86 (Washington D.C.: February 1988).

nance items. This deferred maintenance ranges from repairing or replacing dilapidated irrigation structures to clearing weeds from irrigation ditches. In addition to the deferred maintenance, water users had expressed concern that BIA had been unresponsive in addressing the projects' ongoing operations and maintenance needs.

My testimony today will summarize the findings of our February 2006 report, along with some recent updates. Specifically, I will discuss (1) BIA's estimated deferred maintenance costs for its irrigation projects; (2) shortcomings that we identified in BIA's management of its irrigation projects; and (3) issues we identified that needed to be addressed to determine the long-term direction of BIA's irrigation program. In addition, I will provide information on actions, where applicable, that BIA has taken to address the three recommendations in our February 2006 report.

For our February 2006 report, we collected documentation from BIA headquarters irrigation officials on the 16 irrigation projects, and we visited and collected information from each of BIA's four regional offices that oversee the 16 irrigation projects. We also visited 9 of the 16 projects, where we collected project-specific information from BIA officials and project stakeholders.[3] To examine estimated deferred maintenance costs, we reviewed BIA's lists of deferred maintenance items and cost estimates, as well as the methodology BIA used to develop these lists and estimates. To determine whether management shortcomings existed, we reviewed relevant federal regulations and agency guidance and we analyzed BIA-wide and project-specific management protocols and systems for the 9 projects we visited. Finally, to determine any issues that needed to be addressed to determine the long-term direction of the projects, we reviewed prior studies on BIA's irrigation program, and we discussed the long-term direction of the program with BIA irrigation officials and project stakeholders. A detailed description of our scope and methodology is presented in appendix I of the February 2006 report.

For comparison purposes and to show changes that BIA has made to its estimate of deferred maintenance costs since our February 2006 report, we collected the most recent estimate of deferred maintenance costs from BIA—data for fiscal year 2014 as of September 30, 2014. We did not assess the reliability of the fiscal year 2014 estimate. We also present information on the status of the three recommendations from our report. The report upon which this testimony statement is based was conducted in accordance with generally accepted government auditing standards. Those standards require that we plan and perform the audit to obtain sufficient, appropriate evidence to provide a reasonable basis for our findings and conclusions based on our audit objectives. We believe that the evidence obtained for our report provided a reasonable basis for our findings and conclusions based on our audit objectives.

Background

BIA's irrigation program was initiated in the late 1800s, as part of the Federal Government's Indian assimilation policy, and it was originally designed to provide economic development opportunities for Indians through agriculture. The Act of July 4, 1884, provided the Secretary of the Interior $50,000 for the general development of irrigation on Indian lands.[4] Over the years, Congress continued to pass additional legislation authorizing and funding irrigation facilities on Indian lands.

BIA's irrigation program includes over 100 ''irrigation systems'' and ''irrigation projects'' that irrigate over 750,000 acres primarily across the West. BIA's irrigation systems are nonrevenue-generating facilities that are primarily used for subsistence gardening and are operated and maintained through a collaborative effort, which generally involves other BIA programs, tribes, and water users. In contrast, BIA's 16 irrigation projects that we reported on in our February 2006 report charged their water users an annual operations and maintenance fee to fund the cost of operating and maintaining the project. Most of BIA's irrigation projects have been considered self-supporting through these operations and maintenance fees. The 16 irrigation projects are located on Indian reservations across the agency's Rocky Mountain, Northwest, Southwest, and Western regions (see fig. 1).

---

[3] We selected these projects based on a combination of factors aimed at maximizing our total coverage (over 50 percent of the projects), visiting at least one project in each of the regions where irrigation projects are located, visiting the project with the highest deferred maintenance cost estimate in each region using BIA's fiscal year 2004 data, and visiting what BIA considered to be the three best projects and the five worst projects. Specifically, we visited: (1) the Blackfeet Irrigation Project, (2) the Colorado River Irrigation Project, (3) the Crow Irrigation Project, (4) the Fort Belknap Irrigation Project, (5) the Pine River Irrigation Project, (6) the San Carlos Indian Works Irrigation Project, (7) the San Carlos Joint Works Irrigation Project, (8) the Wapato Irrigation Project, and (9) the Wind River Irrigation Project.
[4] Act of July 4, 1884, 23 Stat. 76, 94 (1884).

Figure 1: Location of the 16 Bureau of Indian Affairs Irrigation Projects Reported on by GAO in February 2006

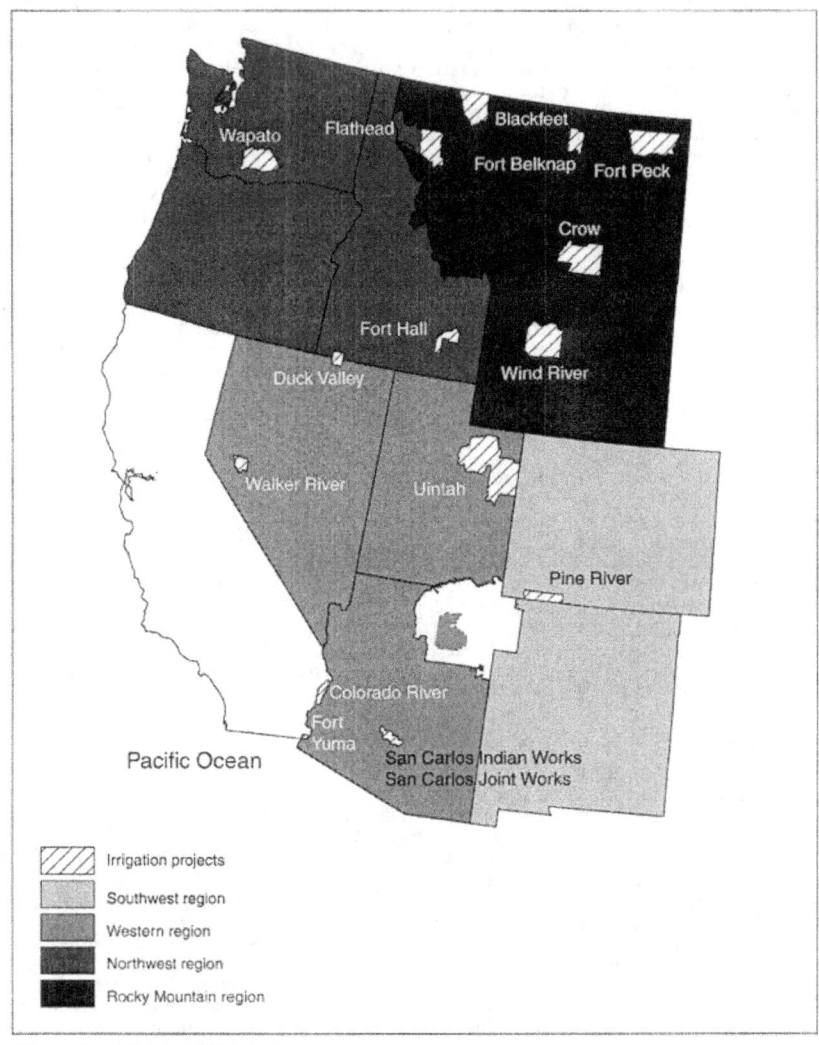

Sources: Bureau of Indian Affairs; GAO. | GAO-15-453T

BIA's management of its irrigation projects was decentralized, with regional and local BIA offices responsible for day-to-day operations and maintenance. Fourteen projects included in our February 2006 report were overseen by local BIA agency superintendents, and the 2 largest projects were overseen directly by regional directors. The local agency superintendents that oversaw these projects reported to their respective regional director. BIA's irrigation and engineering experts, who provide technical assistance to the projects, were located in each region, as well as in BIA's central office located in Washington, D.C., and other BIA locations in the western United States. The regional irrigation staff and central irrigation office staff did not have line authority over the projects.

The irrigation facilities constructed by BIA include a range of structures for storing and delivering water for agricultural purposes. Figure 2 highlights an example of the key structural features found on BIA's irrigation projects.

Figure 2: Example of an Irrigation Project Operated by the Bureau of Indian Affairs

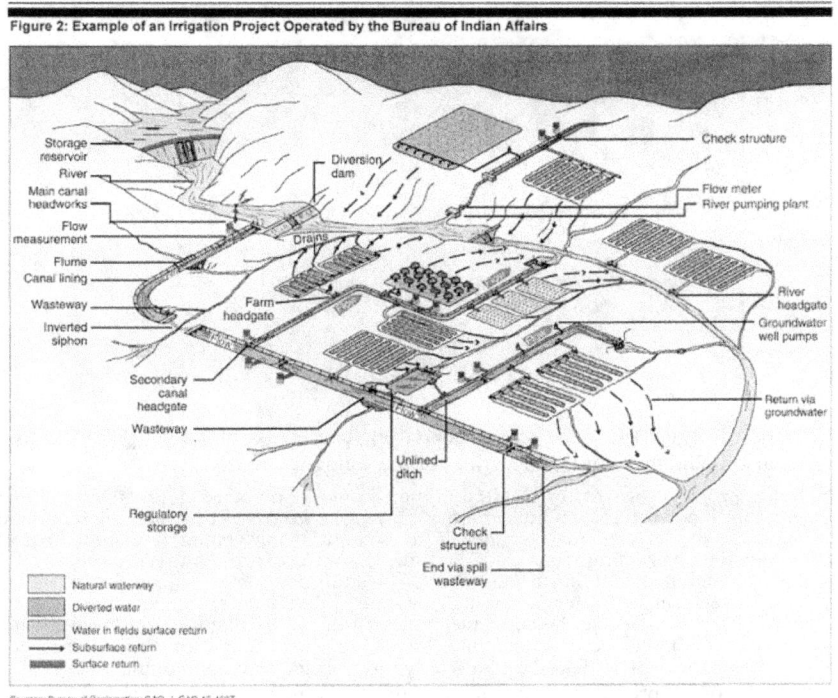

In our February 2006 report,[5] we found that BIA had estimated the cost for deferred maintenance at the 16 irrigation projects at about $850 million for fiscal year 2005. See figure 3 for a breakdown of the cost estimate by project at that time.

BIA Estimated the Cost of Deferred Maintenance at about $850 Million in 2005, but the Estimate Has Since Been Refined to about $570 Million

---

[5]GAO–06–314.

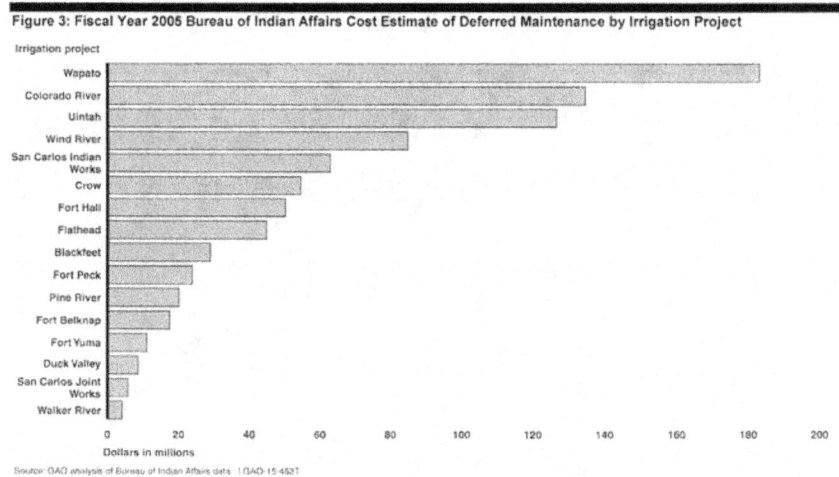

Figure 3: Fiscal Year 2005 Bureau of Indian Affairs Cost Estimate of Deferred Maintenance by Irrigation Project

In 2006, we acknowledged that the $850 million estimate was a work in progress, but we also found that it was inaccurate for the following reasons:

- Some projects incorrectly counted certain items as deferred maintenance. Some projects incorrectly counted certain items, such as new construction items and vehicles, as deferred maintenance. For example, the Wapato Irrigation Project included constructing reservoirs and the San Carlos Indian Works Irrigation Project included building a new office. In addition, some projects included the cost of repairing vehicles or buying new ones in their deferred maintenance estimates, despite BIA guidance at the time of our report that such items were not deferred maintenance. For example, the Wind River Irrigation Project included an excavator vehicle, and the Crow Irrigation Project included dump trucks.

- Some projects provided BIA with incomplete information. According to BIA officials, some projects did not do thorough assessments of their deferred maintenance needs, and some may not have included legitimate deferred maintenance items, such as resloping canal banks that have eroded by crossing cattle or overgrown vegetation. Moreover, neither the Walker River Irrigation Project nor the Uintah Irrigation Project provided information detailing their deferred maintenance costs at the time of our report.

- BIA made errors when compiling the total deferred maintenance cost estimates. For example, BIA inadvertently double-counted the estimate provided by the Colorado River Irrigation Project when compiling the overall cost estimate, according to BIA officials. Additionally, BIA officials erroneously estimated costs for all structures, such as flumes and check gates, based on the full replacement values even when items were in good or fair condition and needed only repairs.

In 2006, we concluded that while the inclusion of incorrect items and calculation errors likely contributed to the overestimation of BIA's total deferred maintenance costs, the incomplete information provided to BIA by some projects may have contributed to the underestimation of the total costs.

As we reported in 2006, to further refine its cost estimate and to develop more comprehensive deferred maintenance lists, BIA planned to hire experts in engineering and irrigation to periodically conduct thorough condition assessments of all 16 irrigation projects to identify deferred maintenance needs and costs. According to BIA officials, these thorough condition assessments were expected to more accurately reflect each project's actual deferred maintenance, in part because experts in engineering and irrigation who can differentiate between structural and cosmetic problems were to conduct them. These assessments were also to help BIA prioritize the allocation of potential funds to complete deferred maintenance items because they would assign a prioritization rating to each deferred maintenance item based on the estimated repair or replacement cost, as well as the overall importance to the project. The first such assessment was completed in July 2005, and BIA planned to reassess the condition of each project at least once every 5 years, with the first round of such condition assessments to be completed by the end of 2010.

While the irrigation projects included in BIA's estimate of deferred maintenance costs have changed somewhat since our report, the most recent deferred maintenance cost estimate for fiscal year 2014 was just under $570 million (see table 1).[6] Several reasons may have contributed to the lower estimate including more thorough condition assessments and maintenance work performed since our report. However, we did not assess the reliability of the fiscal year 2014 estimate.[7] The new estimate is presented for comparison purposes to demonstrate changes that BIA made to the earlier fiscal year 2005 estimate that we raised concerns about in our February 2006 report. Table 1 also shows that most of the condition assessments are now more than 5 years old, and they were not all completed by 2010. Condition assessments for a few projects are still ongoing.

Table 1: Bureau of Indian Affair's Refined Estimate of Deferred Maintenance Costs, Fiscal Year 2014

Dollars in millions

Irrigation project	Deferred maintenance for fiscal year 2014	Condition assessment completion date	Replacement value
Irrigation projects in GAO's February 2006 report, GAO-06-314			
Wapato	$138	2014	$1,971
Flathead	82	2008	237
Fort Hall	30	2009	128
Wind River	30	2008	93
Blackfeet	26	2007	50
Uintah	25	2009	593
Colorado River	17	2011	333
Crow	17	2007	59
Walker River	17	2008	44
San Carlos[a]	16	Ongoing	201
Fort Peck	13	2007	33
Pine River	11	2008	39
Duck Valley	8	2009	48
Fort Belknap	8	2007	19
Fort Yuma	b	b	b
Subtotal	$438		$3,247
Other irrigation real property assets that the Bureau of Indian Affairs counts in its estimate			
Navajo	$125	Ongoing	$1,039
Pyramid Lake	5	Ongoing	49
Subtotal	$130		$1,088
Total	$568		$4,335

Source: Bureau of Indian Affairs. | GAO-15-453T

Notes: We did not assess the reliability of BIA's new estimates, they are presented simply for comparison purposes to demonstrate changes that BIA has made since its fiscal year 2005 estimate.

Some water rights settlements between Indian tribes and the federal government established funds or accounts for irrigation project maintenance, which may be used to fund some or all of the deferred maintenance at those projects. For example, water rights settlements between the federal government and the Crow Tribe and the Shoshone-Paiute Tribes of the Duck Valley Reservation established funds or accounts for maintenance of the Crow and Duck Valley Irrigation Projects, respectively.

[a]In our February 2006 report, we listed the San Carlos Joint Works Irrigation Project and the San Carlos Indian Works Irrigation Project separately. Since February 2006 report, the management of those projects has been reorganized, and the Bureau of Indian Affairs now tracks them together as one project.

[b]Fort Yuma is the responsibility of the Bureau of Reclamation.

BIA Addressed the Management Shortcomings Identified in Our February 2006 Report

In our February 2006 report, we found that BIA's management of some of its irrigation projects had serious shortcomings that undermined effective decisionmaking about project operations and maintenance. First, under BIA's organizational structure, in many cases, officials with the authority to oversee project managers' decisionmaking lacked the technical expertise needed to do so effectively, while the staff who had the expertise lacked the necessary authority to oversee project managers' decisionmaking. The BIA regional directors and local agency superintendents and deputy superintendents that provided oversight on projects did not generally have

---

[6] The fiscal year 2014 and fiscal year 2005 estimates, either by project or in total, cannot be directly compared without adjusting for inflation. In addition, since the number of projects included in each year's total estimate varies, any comparison of the total estimates would not be meaningful.

[7] Specifically, we did not determine the extent to which BIA addressed the inaccuracies that we found in its fiscal year 2005 estimate or whether any such inaccuracies still remain.

engineering or irrigation expertise and relied heavily on the project managers to run the projects. Of the nine projects that we visited for our February 2006 report, only two had managers at the regional or agency levels who were experts in irrigation or engineering. We found that such an organizational structure and reliance on the project managers breaks down when the person managing the project lacks the expertise required for the position—that is, in cases in which BIA has had difficulty filling project manager vacancies and has, as a result, hired less qualified people. For example, at the Crow project in 2002, a project manager with insufficient expertise decided to repair a minor leak in a key water delivery structure by dismantling it and replacing it with a different type of structure. The new structure was subsequently deemed inadequate by BIA's irrigation experts, and the required reconstruction delayed water delivery by about a month. Furthermore, we found that the BIA staff with the necessary expertise—regional irrigation engineers and central irrigation office staff—had no authority over the 16 projects. Consequently, key technical decisions about project operations and maintenance, such as when or how to repair critical water delivery infrastructure, did not necessarily get the technical oversight or scrutiny needed.

To address this shortcoming, in our February 2006 report, we recommended that BIA provide the necessary level of technical support for project managers who have less than the desired level of engineering qualifications by putting these projects under the direct supervision of regional or central irrigation office staff or by implementing more stringent protocols for engineer review and approval of actions taken at the projects. In response to our recommendation, in February 2007, the Director of BIA issued a technical review and assistance policy directive to the relevant BIA regional directors to ensure that adequate review and assistance is given to BIA irrigation project managers. The policy provided for strict protocols for engineer review and approval of actions taken at the projects by those with the necessary engineering expertise. It also outlined specific responsibilities for irrigation project managers, as well as other key irrigation staff. In addition, BIA has made other organizational line authority changes to address this recommendation. [8]

Second, in our February 2006 report, we found that BIA did not consistently provide information and opportunities for stakeholders to participate in setting project priorities. Federal regulations required BIA to consult with project stakeholders—such as, tribal council representatives, as well as Indian and non-Indian water users—in setting project priorities but BIA did not consistently do so.9 For example, we reported that the Wapato Irrigation Project had shared little information on its spending with stakeholders, and the Pine River Irrigation Project did not meet with its nontribal stakeholders, limiting stakeholders' ability to have an impact on project decisions and BIA's ability to benefit from their input.

925 C.F.R. § 171.1(c) (2005). This regulation was amended in 2008 to require BIA to cooperate and consult with all interested parties, especially persons or entities to which it provides irrigation service and receives uses of BIA irrigation facilities, such as irrigators and landowners. 25 C.F.R. § 171.110(b) (2015).

To address the second shortcoming, in our February 2006 report, we recommended that BIA require, at a minimum, that irrigation project management meet twice annually with all project stakeholders—once at the end of a season and once before the next season—to provide information on project operations, including budget plans and actual annual expenditures, and to obtain feedback and input. In response to our recommendation, in July 2006, the Acting Director of BIA directed each of the four BIA regional directors responsible for the 16 irrigation projects to personally ensure that irrigation staff meet twice annually, at a minimum, with water users and other stakeholders—once at the end of the season and once before the next season. For projects that operate year-round, the project managers in consultation with project water users were to determine mutually acceptable times for holding these two annual meetings. At these meetings, BIA's irrigation project managers and irrigation staff were directed to provide information on project operations, including budget plans and actual annual expenditures, and obtain feedback and input. This policy change was published in the Federal Register in April 2007. [10] In addition, BIA irrigation project managers were directed to submit documentation of the meetings to BIA headquarters irrigation staff.

---

[8] For example, according to BIA, the Rocky Mountain Region realigned the organizational structure for its five irrigation projects. The five Irrigation Project Managers now report directly to the Regional Water Resources Branch Chief, an engineering position.

[10] 72 Fed. Reg. 19950 (Apr. 20, 2007).

Long-Term Direction of BIA's Irrigation Program Depends on Resolution of a Number of Larger Issues

In our February 2006 report, we found that the long-term direction of BIA's irrigation program depended on the resolution of the following larger issues:

- *Financial sustainability.* Of the most importance, BIA did not know to what extent its irrigation projects were capable of financially sustaining themselves, which hindered the agency's ability to address long-standing concerns regarding inadequate funding. Despite this lack of information on the overall financial situation for each of the projects, in the early 1960s, BIA classified more than half of the 16 projects that we reported on as fully self-supporting on the basis of annual operations and maintenance fees they collected from water users. These self-supporting projects did not receive any ongoing appropriated funds. These projects were subject to full cost recovery despite the absence of financial information to demonstrate that the water users could sustain this financial burden. The heavy reliance on water users to sustain these projects had created ongoing tension between the water users and BIA. Some water users had complained to BIA that they could not afford the operations and maintenance fees, and they had pressured BIA to keep the fees as low as possible. Without definitive information on the financial situation of each project, we concluded that BIA could not determine what portion of project operations and maintenance costs can be reasonably borne by the water users and to what extent alternative sources of financing, such as congressional appropriations, should be pursued.

- *Funding for deferred maintenance.* The future of BIA's irrigation program also depended on the resolution of how the deferred maintenance will be funded. BIA did not have a plan for how it would obtain funding to fix the deferred maintenance items. Regardless of the precise cost estimate for total deferred maintenance, we concluded that funding deferred maintenance costs in the hundreds of millions of dollars will be a significant challenge in times of tight budgets and competing priorities.

- *Alternative project managers.* Given that BIA must balance irrigation management with its many other missions in support of Indian communities, such as providing education and law enforcement, we reported that there were inherent limits on the resources and knowledge that BIA was able to devote to any one program. As a result of these limitations and competing demands, officials told us at the time of our report that irrigation management is not a priority for BIA. In our February 2006 report, we found that it may be beneficial to consider whether others for whom irrigation is more of a priority or an area of expertise, including other federal agencies, Indian tribes, and water users, could better manage some of the projects. We concluded that successful management of the projects by others, however, would depend on the characteristics of each project and its stakeholders. For example, turning over projects to tribes may be an option for projects where most of the water users are Indian, whereas turning over projects to water users may be an option for projects where water users share similar interests and have a desire to organize into an irrigation district or association.

To obtain information on the long-term financial sustainability of each of the projects, we recommended in our February 2006 report that BIA conduct studies to determine both how much it would cost to financially sustain each project, and the extent to which water users on each project have the ability to pay these costs. [11] We stated that this information would be useful to congressional decision makers and other interested parties in debating the long-term direction of BIA's irrigation program. However, to date, BIA has not implemented this recommendation. In June 2008, the Department of the Interior provided us with a memorandum that stated, while the department agreed that studies to assess the financial sustainability of the irrigation projects would be valuable, it did not have sufficient funding to perform these studies—and does not expect to have such funding in the foreseeable future.

In conclusion, BIA irrigation projects continue to face hundreds of millions of dollars of deferred maintenance needs. The Senate bill, S. 438, if enacted, could help address these needs and potentially some of the other larger issues that we reported on in our February 2006 report. By establishing an Indian Irrigation Fund for fiscal years 2015 through 2036, this bill, if enacted, would help provide needed resources to carry out maintenance, repair, and replacement activities for certain Indian irri-

---

[11] GAO–06–314.

gation projects and funds to conduct a study of BIA's Indian irrigation program and project management.

Chairman Barrasso, Vice Chairman Tester, and Members of the Committee, this completes my prepared statement. I would be pleased to answer any questions that you may have at this time.

The CHAIRMAN. Thank you very much, Ms. Fennell.

Next, we will hear from the Honorable Charles Headdress of Montana.

STATEMENT OF HON. CHARLES HEADDRESS, SR., COUNCILMAN, ASSINIBOINE AND SIOUX TRIBES, FORT PECK RESERVATION

Mr. HEADDRESS. Thank you.

Good afternoon, Chairman Barrasso and Vice Chairman Tester.

My name is Charles Headdress. I am a member of the Fort Peck Tribal Executive Board. I want to thank you both for introducing and holding this hearing on S. 438, the IRRIGATE Act.

Fort Peck Reservation encompasses 2.1 million acres, over 2,000 square miles in northeastern Montana. The tribes and individual Indian allottees own about 1 million acres of land on the reservation. The development of the irrigation project for the Fort Peck Reservation was a key part of the plan and obligation that the Federal Government assumed when it established our reservation.

After our reservation was created, the Federal Government, using military force, prohibited our people from leaving the reservation to hunt. Without the ability to hunt, we could not meet our basic needs. The government wanted us to be farmers, but reservation resources were not sufficient to do this.

After several years of drought and starvation among our people, the government recognized the need to develop irrigation so that we might survive by agriculture. The Fort Peck Irrigation Project was authorized by a 1908 Act that required the Bureau of Reclamation to construct the Fort Peck irrigation system.

The project was planned with the intent of irrigating up to 152,000 acres of land. Unfortunately, this never came to be. Instead, the Fort Peck Reservation Irrigation Project consists of two irrigation units, the Wyoming unit and the Frazer-Wolf Point Unit.

Together, these units can only irrigate 18,953 acres, approximately 12 percent of what was initially planned to serve my reservation. The critics stated the Fort Peck system was a waste and poor.

The national backlog of deferred maintenance on the irrigation projects is in excess of $600 million. According to the BIA's 2014 Deferred Maintenance Report, the backlog of deferred maintenance for the Fort Peck Project is $12.7 million.

The impact of this deferred maintenance on the economy of the Fort Peck tribes cannot be understated. The income generated by the farming and grazing has been a mainstay for the tribes and tribal members. The revenue generated from grazing and agricultural leasing of trust land is on average 30–50 percent of the tribe's total trust income.

The repair and restoration of the irrigation project is also key to creating jobs. The Fort Peck Reservation's unemployment rate has hovered above 50 percent for most of the last two decades. Poverty among our members remains at epidemic levels as illustrated by the fact that more than 80 percent of our children are eligible for free or reduced price school lunches.

We have to do more to put our people to work and lift our children out of poverty. It is time for Congress to fulfill the original promise of the 1908 Act to make our reservation self-supporting.

As the Committee moves forward with this legislation, the tribes ask that the legislation be amended in three ways. First, Congress must clarify the use of these funds to repair these tribal irrigation projects is not a reimbursable expense to be levied against the project users.

In the past, when money was appropriated to repair tribal irrigation projects, the department deemed it to be reimbursable and levied additional assessments against the users.

Second, the unpaid construction debt on the Fort Peck Reservation system is $7 million. Demanding repayment of this debt is not realistic. While the Secretary has the authority to forgive this debt, our pleas have fallen on deaf ears. We urge Congress to act now to forgive this debt.

Finally, we ask that this bill be amended to include the Rural Water Projects Completion Act to complete the drinking water systems authorized by Congress. These projects include the Fort Peck Reservation rural water system and the Rocky Boys North Central Project.

The fate of our reservations rests on the health of our people and the health of our people depends on the water we drink. Thus, I would urge the Committee, as you take up this bill, to amend it to include provisions that would also ensure these rural water projects can be completed on time.

I would like to thank you for your time and your interest in this vitally important matter. I would be happy to answer any questions.

[The prepared statement of Mr. Headdress follows:]

PREPARED STATEMENT OF HON. CHARLES HEADDRESS, SR., COUNCILMAN, ASSINIBOINE AND SIOUX TRIBES, FORT PECK RESERVATION

Good afternoon Chairman Barrasso and Vice-Chairman Tester. My name is Charles Headdress, Sr., and I am member of the Fort Peck Tribal Executive Board, the governing body of the Assiniboine and Sioux Tribes of the Fort Peck Reservation. I want to thank you for holding this hearing on S. 438, the Irrigation Rehabilitation and Renovation for Indian Tribal Governments and their Economies (IRRIGATE) Act. I also want to express my appreciation for two of the bill's co-sponsors: Senator Tester for the invitation to testify today; and Montana's junior Senator Steve Daines for his interest on this important subject and in serving on this important Committee.

The Fort Peck Reservation encompasses 2.1 million acres—over two thousand square miles—in remote northeastern Montana. The Assiniboine and Sioux Tribes and individual Indian allottees own about 1 million acres of land on the Reservation. Nearly 10,000 people live on the Reservation, of which roughly two-thirds are Tribal members and non-member Indians.

The development of an irrigation project for the Fort Peck Reservation was an integral element of the plan and obligation that the Federal Government assumed when it established our Reservation. After our Reservation was created, the Federal Government, using military force, prohibited our people from leaving the Reservation to hunt the game on which we historically depended to meet all of our most basic needs. The government instead sought to have us engage in farming and ranching. But the Reservation resources were not sufficient to do this. After several years of drought and starvation among our people, the government recognized the need to develop irrigation so that we might, in fact, survive by agriculture.

The Fort Peck Irrigation Project was formally authorized by the Act of May 30, 1908. Importantly, pursuant to this 1908 Act, it was the Bureau of Reclamation that was charged with direct responsibility for materials, workmanship, and economy of construction of the irrigation system. Congress recognized that the Bureau of Indian Affairs did not have the capability of constructing the kind of irrigation project that was needed at Fort Peck. When Congress enacted this legislation it intended to provide the Fort Peck Tribes with the means to become selfsupporting through the development of agricultural and grazing lands. Accordingly, the project was planned with the intent of irrigating up to 152,000 acres of land. Unfortunately, for a number of reasons associated with various failed federal policies—including allotment, removal of children from homes (which impeded the ability to run family farms, as there were no families), and the levying of construction debt against trust prop- erty—this never came to be.

Instead today, the Fort Peck Reservation Irrigation Project consists of two irrigation units: the Wiota Unit and Frazer-Wolf Point Unit. Together these units irrigate only 18,953 acres, approximately 12 percent of what was initially planned to serve my Reservation to meet the needs of my people. Out of these 18,953 acres, only 9,758 acres remain in trust, with the other 9,195 acres held in fee status. Some of the fee lands are owned by Tribal members.

The current condition of the Fort Peck Reservation Irrigation System is worse than poor. The national backlog of deferred maintenance on irrigation projects is in excess of $600 million. According to the BIA's 2014 Q4 Deferred Maintenance Report, the total backlog deferred maintenance for the Fort Peck Project is $12.7 million.

The impact of this deferred maintenance on the economy of the Fort Peck Tribes cannot be understated. Throughout the history of the Reservation the income generated by the farming and grazing has been a mainstay for the Tribes and Tribal members. Even in the years when there was an oil and gas boom for the Reservation, the revenue generated from grazing and agricultural leasing of the Tribes' trust lands was still approximately 30–50 percent of the Tribes' total trust income. In more recent years, where revenues from oil and gas have declined, the agricultural revenues are at the heart of funding Tribal government operations, programs, and services that are so critically needed by our people. The repair and restoration of the irrigation system is also key to creating jobs. The Fort Peck Reservation's unemployment rate has hovered above 50 percent for most of the last two decades. Poverty among our members remains at epidemic levels, as illustrated by the fact that more than 80 percent of our children are eligible for free or reduced-price school lunch. We have to do more to put our people to work and lift our children out of poverty. It is time for Congress to fulfill the original promise of the 1908 Act to make our Reservation self-supporting.

Thus, the Fort Peck Tribes stand in support of the IRRIGATE Act. This Act will address the $600 million tribal irrigation maintenance and repair backlog by allocating from the Reclamation Fund, $35 million each year from 2015 through 2036, into a new account in the Treasury called the Indian Irrigation Fund.

For those who might say this is not an appropriate use of the Reclamation Fund, we would like to correct them. The use of the Reclamation Fund to repair the Fort Peck Irrigation Project is entirely appropriate and is in fact, exactly the purpose for which the Reclamation Fund was established. The Fort Peck Project was originally developed as a Reclamation Project. The fact that the project could not generate revenues necessary to maintain itself is a consequence of Reclamation's failure to do its job right in the first place.

In this regard, the Tribes ask that the legislation be clarified to state that use of these funds to repair these Tribal irrigation projects is not a reimbursable expense. In the past, when money was appropriated to repair tribal irrigation projects, the Department deemed it to be reimbursable and levied additional assessments against the users. Currently, the unpaid construction debt on Fort Peck Reservation system is $7 million. Almost two decades ago, the Bureau of Reclamation did an analysis of the users' payment capacity and found it to be $15.50 per acre ($14.00 in O&M and $1.50 in construction repayment). Those figures would have meant it would have taken 250 years to satisfy the construction debt. Demanding repayment was not realistic then and it is not realistic now. We do not believe you intend the funds to be provided by the IRRIGATE Act to be added to the Project's construction debt, but given the Department's past positions, we urge that the legislation make clear that the funds provided are not to be subject to repayment by the users.

Moreover, to ensure the viability of the Fort Peck Project, we urge Congress to forgive the existing project debt. The amount of idle acreage continues to increase because landowners and potential lessees cannot afford to bring the debt current to get water delivered to the property. This both leaves the land idle, and decreases its value. As a consequence the Fort Peck Project is under-serving the intended project area. Even more troubling, we have heard from fractionated landowners within the Project that the government has become increasingly aggressive in seeking to recover Project debt. The Tribes at Fort Peck have been urging Congress to address this unfairness since 1993. While the Secretary has the authority to forgive this debt, our pleas have fallen on deaf ears. Congress has forgiven irrigation project debt in the past, including past debt for the Fort Peck Project, and we urge Congress to act now to forgive the current debt.

Beyond strengthening our tribal economy, repairing this project and addressing its debt would help preserve our resources. We are all aware of the need to use our resources efficiently, and there is no natural resource more precious to our people than water. This is especially true when the West is facing some of the worst droughts this Nation has ever experienced. By repairing and maintaining this Project, we will be ensuring that the water resources that the Fort Peck Tribes have fought so hard to protect are used wisely and efficiently.

In this regard, last Congress both the Chairman and the Vice-Chairman supported a similar bill in the Senate, the Rural Water Projects Completion Act, which was approved by the Senate Energy and Natural Resources Committee. Senator Daines introduced a companion bill during his tenure in the House. In addition to addressing the irrigation project maintenance and repair backlog, these bills would have created a mechanism to complete the several Rural Water Projects that have been authorized by Congress. These Projects include the Fort Peck Reservation Rural Water System and the Rocky Boy's North Central Project. The fate of our Reservations rests on the health of our people, and the health of our people depends on the water we drink. I know that Senator Tester knows this. There is probably no other United States Senator who cannot drink the water that comes from his kitchen sink, but I know that is the case for Senator Tester. Thus, I would urge the Committee as you take up this bill to follow the leadership of Senators Tester and Daines to amend it to include provisions that would also ensure that these rural water projects can be completed on time.

I would like to thank you for your time and interest in this vitally important matter, and I would be happy to answer any questions.

Supplemental Testimony

On behalf of the Fort Peck Tribes, we again want to thank you for introducing S. 438, the IRRIGATE Act, and holding a hearing on this important measure. We also very much appreciate having the opportunity to testify at the hearing. We write to supplement the testimony that we submitted and to provide additional information in response to the questions raised during the hearing.

What the irrigation project means for Fort Peck today and how important it and agriculture are for economic development at Fort Peck. The Irrigation Project and agriculture generally are a central part of our economy. This is so for several reasons:

First, a working irrigation project provides direct employment to the families who own the land within the irrigation project and who are running farms on that land.

Second, a working irrigation project not only benefits the families that are actually irrigating the land, but also many tribal members who own interests in trust land within the project and who lease those lands to farmers. Even where trust lands are fractionated, the rent paid on the leases of those lands is an important source of income to tribal members.

Third, the lands that are irrigated are used to grow alfalfa and hay, which—in turn—helps support the livestock industry on other parts of the Reservation. Many tribal members are ranchers who buy hay from the irrigators and others. In some years, if there is drought in other parts of the country, the market for hay is very good and hay grown at Fort Peck has been sold to ranchers outside the Reservation. We estimate that about 30 percent of Tribal members make their living from farming and ranching.

Fourth, income from farming and grazing is a very large portion of the Tribes' budget. Even in the years when we had an oil and gas boom on the Reservation, income from farming and grazing leases was between 30 percent and 50 percent of Tribal revenues. Today, income from these leases is even a bigger portion of our Tribal income. That money is then used to help pay for our government programs and services and to employ many tribal members who work for the Tribes.

In short, agriculture has direct and indirect benefits for essentially all of the 10,000 people who live on our Reservation, approximately 8,000 of whom are Tribal members and other Indians.

The current condition of the project. There are 18,953 acres of land within the Fort Peck Irrigation Project. Approximately 10 percent of the land within the project is not productive and the backlog of deferred maintenance is a factor which contributes to this.

The limited funding available to repair and maintain Indian Irrigation Projects means that maintenance is not done until elements of the project are at risk of complete failure. That is what has occurred at Fort Peck. We were fortunate that last year a portion of the BIA's Irrigation Projects-Rehabilitation Program funds were allocated to repair portions of the Frazer and Wiota Pump Stations. But this occurred in large part because of the serious deterioration of those stations. The need for repairs to these pump stations had been a high priority for close to 10 years before the funds became available. As set out in the President's Budget for FY 2015 released in January 2014, the Frazer Pump Station is 40 years old and three of the four pumps have exceeded their expected service life. The outlet pipes are severely corroded and on the verge of compromising the entire system. There are also significant safety issues surrounding the entire system, and 13,000 acres of farmland would not be irrigated at all if this pump station were inoperable. The funds allocated last year are now being used to address part of these problems. We were able to install one new pump in the Frazer Station and one new pump in the Wiota Station, along with the related electric work for each and some work on the outlet pipes.

But additional work still remains to be done. The other pumps at these stations are old, so while they are still working, they are still past the expected service life. There is constant need to maintain canals, laterals and ditches. Many of these have considerable overgrowth of vegetation, and many of the concrete structures are cracked and deteriorating. We also see significant silt buildup which has become worse over time. Some years ago there were fingers of riprap, rock and other material on the other side of the river which accelerated the river flow and limited the silt deposit. But those fingers have worn out and we have since seen considerable buildup of silt which we will need to remove.

In addition, the low levels of water in the river means that we often have high growth of moss which then gets caught in and threatens to clog the intakes of the pumping stations. To prevent clogged intakes (which would jam and burn-out the pumps and threaten stress cracks in the structure), we have had to have staff, in boats, manually remove moss from the intakes. This activity is highly dangerous, as river currents are pushing the boat into the intakes and we had one near drowning last year. There is equipment that could do this work automatically—but the cost, based on estimates a few years ago, was $100,000 per bay, with the Frazer Pumping Station and Wiota Pumping Station having a combined total of seven bays. There are no funds to acquire this equipment.

The adverse impact of reimbursable construction costs on the Tribes and individual landowners. During the hearing, we explained that the Interior Department's demands that trust landowners repay construction debt which has been assessed against the trust property has created a substantial problem for both tribal members and the Tribes. When the federal government undertook to develop irrigation projects on Indian reservations in the late 1800s and early 1900s, congressional policy regarding the costs of such projects varied. On some reservations, the costs of construction were initially to be paid simply out of appropriated federal funds. For others, however, the authorizing statute directed that the costs be reimbursed out of tribal funds. Beginning in 1914, Congress directed that construction costs for all such projects be paid by the persons who owned land served by the irrigation project. However, these acts were not enforced against non-Indians who had purchased allotments and acquired vested rights in the land prior to the statutes' effective dates, although construction costs were still assessed against Indian lands. [1]

Indians could not pay these costs, and many of the irrigation projects that were built—including several at Fort Peck—proved not to be viable due to irregular and undependable water supplies and were later abandoned. Indeed, at Fort Peck it was not until 1940, with the construction of the Fort Peck Dam on the Missouri River, that there was a certain enough water supply to allow for effective implementation of the irrigation units that remain today.

In 1932, Congress recognized the inequities of seeking to recover construction costs from Indians and enacted the Leavitt Act to relieve Indians of liability for construction costs and defer assessment of all future construction costs so long as the lands remained in Indian ownership. 47 Stat. 564 codified at 25 U.S.C. 386a. In 1936, another act of Congress authorized the Secretary of the Interior to investigate

---

[1] This history is summarized in Felix S. Cohen's Handbook of Federal Indian Law at 729–730 (1982 ed.)

whether the owners of non-Indian lands within Indian irrigation projects are unable to pay irrigation charges, including construction costs, and to adjust defer or cancel such charges. Act of June 22, 1936, 49 Stat. 1803, codified at 25 U.S.C. 389–389e.

While a portion of the original construction costs assessed against the Fort Peck Irrigation Project were cancelled under these acts,[2] part of those charges remain and continue to be liens against trust and fee lands. In more recent years, the Secretary has relied on the early statutes to conclude that other federal funds appropriated to repair or rehabilitate the projects are to be assessed against and reimbursed from the landowners. For example, in 1990, when Congress appropriated $995,000 for rehabilitation and betterment of the Indian Irrigation Projects, including the Fort Peck Irrigation Project, those construction costs were assessed against the landowners and, although collection of the charges were deferred as to trust lands, those costs are, nevertheless liens against the trust property. *See Fort Peck Water-users Association v. Billings Area Director,* BIA, 26 IBIA 90 (1994).

One of the complications presented by the outstanding liens on the property is their impact of the Land Buyback Program. The Fort Peck Tribes are trying to re-purchase the fractioned interests through that program, but for fractioned trust lands that are within the Irrigation Project, the liens create significant additional issues. These liens impact the appraisals required under the Buyback Program. Where there is outstanding debt and the land has been out of production, there are questions about whether it should be appraised simply as dryland (at a much lower value) or for its potential as irrigated lands. In addition, even when outstanding debts are repaid so that the land can be irrigated, work often needs to be done to put the land back into a condition where irrigation will be effective.

It has not yet been possible to maintain the Fort Peck Irrigation Project through the claims for reimbursement of construction costs and assessment of O&M charges. The failure to determine the feasibility of such projects at the time of their original construction, to keep records necessary to properly allocate costs, and to do the work needed to properly maintain these projects, has prevented irrigation projects like that at Fort Peck from becoming self-sustaining. The outstanding debts, in turn, have resulted in a vicious cycle where lack of adequate funds to maintain and repair the irrigation systems leads to increasing amounts of deferred maintenance, which over time, means that land within the irrigation project is not productively used. And as more land is out of production, less can be paid in O&M charges, thereby compounding the backlog of deferred maintenance.

Forgiving the existing debt would make a major difference. At a minimum, however, S. 438 should include express language that the funds made available under it not be reimbursable. The funding authorized by S. 438 should be used to address the deferred maintenance on terms that create a fresh start—so that these projects can be brought back to working condition and the landowners given the opportunity to move forward without the burdens of repaying costs of repair and rehabilitation that have become so large as a result of past failed policies.

We do not believe that the sponsors of S. 438 intended that the funds authorized by this bill be reimbursable from the landowners. When the substantive provisions of this bill were considered last year (in S. 715), and OMB scored those provisions, OMB treated these funds as non-reimbursable. See S. Rept. No. 113–167 at 12 (2014). However, given the Department's policies in implementing the other federal laws that can bear on these projects, a clear statement in this legislation, that the costs are not reimbursable, is important.

The possibility of expanding the current irrigation system. The Fort Peck Tribes welcome all opportunities to improve our community and develop our economy. Water is an integral part of that. Over the years, the Tribes have identified additional locations that, based on feasibility studies, are good candidates for irrigation projects within the Reservation. One such project is a potential pivot irrigation system in Fort Kipp that has access to the Missouri River and would cover 2,300 acres. Another potential pivot irrigation system is in an area known as North of Sprole, which is just east of Poplar. This project, if developed, could irrigate approximately

---

[2] For example, following enactment of the Leavitt Act, the Secretary cancelled only $430,278 of construction and O&M costs assessed against the Fort Peck Project, on the assumption that the landowners could repay the remaining $581,530 in construction costs then assessed against the project. H. Doc. No. 72–501 at 16–18, 27–38 (1932). In 1967, Congress approved a Secretarial order cancelling $206,902 in reimbursable construction costs, as well as $118,266 in unassessed construction costs allocable against both Indian and non-Indian owned lands at Fort Peck. P. L. No. 90–143, Nov. 16, 1967, 81 Stat. 465. The cancelled costs were a portion of the outstanding costs that related to a) irrigation units that no longer functioned, b) costs incurred but not attributed to any specific lands within the project, and c) part of the costs assessed against non-Indian landowners to equalize the charges with those assessed against Indian lands. S. Rept. No. 90–691 (1967); H.R. Rept. No. 90–748 (1967).

15,000 acres of land of which 42 percent are tribal, 30 percent are allotted and 28 percent are fee. We think expanding irrigation on the Reservation will bring positive results and move toward fulfilling promises that have been long forgotten.

Conclusion. Again, we want to express our sincere appreciation to this Committee for its commitment and work on this important matter.

The CHAIRMAN. Thank you very much, Mr. Headdress. I appreciate you being here.

Our next witness is Mitchel T. Cottenoir, Tribal Water Engineer, Shoshone and Arapaho Tribes of the Wind River Reservation, Fort Washakie, Wyoming. Thanks so much for joining us.

STATEMENT OF MITCHEL T. COTTENOIR, TRIBAL WATER ENGINEER, EASTERN SHOSHONE AND NORTHERN ARAPAHO TRIBES, WIND RIVER RESERVATION

Mr. COTTENOIR. Chairman Barrasso, Vice Chairman Tester and members of the Committee, thank you for inviting me as a representative of the Eastern Shoshone and Northern Arapaho Tribes to appear before you today.

The condition of the Wind River Irrigation Project, as well as numerous other Bureau of Indian Affairs operated irrigation systems, is well documented. The Wind River Irrigation Project was authorized for construction in 1905 but was never completed.

Since that time, the project, under the operation of the BIA, has been neglected to the extent that the cost to rehabilitate and complete the system is estimated in the range of $30-$90 million.

The Wind River Irrigation Project is significantly under staffed and has operated inefficiently with only minor necessary maintenance. The BIA continues to not have a long term plan for rehabilitation of the Wind River Irrigation Project.

Therefore, the Eastern Shoshone and the Northern Arapaho Tribes, the Wind River Water Resource Control Board and the Office of the Tribal Water Engineer have undertaken a major rehabilitation effort to rehabilitate aging structures crucial to the operation of the system.

The tribes have utilized Federal appropriations acquired through the efforts led by Senator Mike Enzi in 2005 and 2006 totaling $3.72 million and leveraged them with State of Wyoming funding through the Wyoming Water Development Commission to rehabilitate 15 major structures in the system at a cost of $7.7 million.

In further effort to provide the required operational and maintenance needs of the system, the tribes have encouraged irrigators to form water user associations. These associations have negotiated cooperative assistance agreements with the Bureau of Indian Affairs to assume the operation and maintenance of their designated portion of the system.

A percentage of the irrigation assessment is returned to the association to provide funding for operations, staff and needed maintenance. Under the CAAs, each association has seen a dramatic improvement in the overall operation and maintenance in their part of the system compared to the past service provided by the BIA.

In addition, the tribes have initiated an effort to assume the operation and maintenance responsibilities of the system under the Indian Self Determination Act, Public Law 93–638. This action would empower the tribes to operate the system more efficiently and effectively. Rehabilitation will become a priority rather than an afterthought.

This effort has also been encouraged by agency and regional level BIA water source management.

With these two strategies, the Bureau of Indian Affairs would be eliminated from the equation. This leaves us with the responsibility to operate, maintain and rehabilitate an aging and deteriorating system on the Wind River.

The tribes have compiled a proven track record and have demonstrated the ability to move the rehabilitation effort forward for the benefit of not only tribal members but our non-tribal neighbors.

Funds that would become available through S. 438, the IRRIGATE Act, would enable the tribes to continue this effort. The IRRIGATE Act could be utilized to leverage funds from the Wyoming Water Development Commission. In doing so, this could expedite the much needed rehabilitation and completion of the Wind River Irrigation Project which has for so long been neglected by the Bureau of Indian Affairs.

Senator Barrasso, Vice Chairman Tester and members of the Committee, the funding from this bill is simply vital to our efforts. We realize that only through our efforts and yours will this absolutely essential rehabilitation occur. Not only can we do this, we must do this.

Senator Barrasso, the Eastern Shoshone and the Northern Arapaho Tribes, the Wind River Water Resource Control Board and the Office of the Tribal Water Engineer strongly endorse S. 438, the Irrigation Rehabilitation and Renovation for Indian Tribal Governments and Their Economies Act or the IRRIGATE Act, as we did with S. 715 when the Barrasso amendment was added in the previous Congress.

We also encourage members of the Committee to do all in their power in moving the IRRIGATE Act forward successfully. The Eastern Shoshone and Northern Arapaho Tribes look forward to working closely with you now and in the future.

Thank you for your time and consideration.

[The prepared statement of Mr. Cottenoir follows:]

PREPARED STATEMENT OF MITCHEL T. COTTENOIR, TRIBAL WATER ENGINEER, EASTERN SHOSHONE AND NORTHERN ARAPAHO TRIBES, WIND RIVER RESERVATION

Chairman Barrasso, Vice Chairman Tester and members of the Committee, thank you for inviting me as a representative of the Eastern Shoshone and Northern Arapaho Tribes to appear before you today.

The condition of the Wind River Irrigation Project, as well as numerous other Bureau of Indian Affairs operated irrigation systems, is well documented. The Wind River Irrigation Project was authorized for construction in 1905, but was never completed. Since that time the project, under the operation of the BIA, has been neglected to the extent that the cost to rehabilitate and complete the system is estimated in the range of $30–$90 million.

Bureau of Indian Affairs Irrigation at the Wind River is significantly understaffed and the system is operated inefficiently with only minor necessary maintenance.

The BIA continues to not have a long term plan for rehabilitation of the Wind River Irrigation Project. Therefore, the Eastern Shoshone and Northern Arapaho Tribes, the Wind River Water Resource Control Board and the Office of the Tribal Water Engineer have undertaken a major rehabilitation effort to rehabilitate aging structures that are crucial to the operation of the system.

To further provide the required operational and maintenance needs of the system the Tribes have encouraged irrigators in the system to form water users associations. These associations have negotiated Cooperative Assistance Agreements (CAA)

with the Bureau of Indian Affairs to assume the operation and maintenance of their designated portion of the system. A percentage of the irrigation assessment is returned to the association to provide funding for operating staff and needed maintenance. Under the CAA each association has seen a dramatic improvement the overall operation and maintenance of their part of the system compared to the past services provided by the Bureau of Indian Affairs.

It is hoped that each association can accumulate a rehabilitation fund to assist in the rehabilitation effort and that can be leveraged to acquire additional funding from sources such as the Wyoming Water Development Commission (WWDC). We have had some success in such efforts in recent years.

In addition, the Tribes have initiated an effort to assume the Operation and Maintenance responsibilities from the BIA under the Indian Self-determination Act PL 93–638. This action would empower the Tribes to operate the system more efficiently and effectively. Rehabilitation would become a priority rather than an afterthought. This effort has also been encouraged by Agency and Regional Level Bureau of Indian Affairs Water Resource management.

With these two strategies, the Bureau of Indian Affairs is eliminated from the equation. It leaves us with the responsibility to operate, maintain and rehabilitate the aging and deteriorating system on the Wind River.

The Eastern Shoshone and Northern Arapaho Tribes, the Wind River Water Resource Control Board and the Office of the Tribal Water Engineer strongly endorse S. 438, the Irrigation Rehabilitation and Renovation for Indian Tribal Governments and Their Economies Act or the "IRRIGATE Act". The funds through this bill would provide for the much needed rehabilitation of the Wind River Irrigation Project that has for decades been neglected by the Bureau of Indian Affairs. The Eastern Shoshone and Northern Arapaho Tribes ask for your individual support in successfully moving the bill forward.

The Tribes have compiled a proven track record and have demonstrated the ability to move the rehabilitation effort forward for the benefit of not only Tribal members, but also our non-tribal neighbors. Funds that would become available to the Tribes through the IRRIGATE Act would enable the Tribes to continue this effort. The IRRIGATE Act funding could be utilized to leverage funding from the State of Wyoming and the WWDC. Tribal participation in this program was allowed for under the 2003 Wyoming State Legislature House Bill 144. In doing so, this could expedite the much needed rehabilitation and completion of the Wind River Irrigation Project which has so long been neglected by the Bureau of Indian Affairs.

In 2004 in an effort to facilitate the rehabilitation of the Wind River Irrigation Project, the Eastern Shoshone and Northern Arapaho Tribes through the efforts of the Wind River Water Resource Control Board applied to and were granted a $3.5M grant from the WWDC to aid in the rehabilitation of irrigation structures that were critical to the operation of the system. This State Appropriation was a 50 percent grant that required an additional $3.5M in matching funds before the State funds could be used. Through the efforts of the Wind River Water Resource Control Board in conjunction with the efforts led by Senator Mike Enzi, a Federal appropriation of $3.72M was secured in 2005 and 2006 as matching funds for the $3.5M in State funds.

These funding sources were utilized to rehabilitate 15 major structures that were crucial to the operation of the irrigation system. These structures include: the Johnstown and Lefthand Ditch diversion and waste-way structures on the Big Wind River, the Coolidge Canal—Trout Creek diversion structure, the Mill Creek—Ray Canal Crossing structure, the Ray Canal—South Fork of the Little Wind diversion structure, the Coolidge Canal—Little Wind diversion structure, Ray Canal 11C, 39C and 59C diversion structures, Coolidge Canal 14B diversion structure, the Sub-agency Canal—Little Wind River diversion structure, the North Fork of the Little Wind River diversion chute structure, and the Willow Creek and Meadow Creek diversion structures in the Crowheart area.

Incorporated in the design and construction of the Coolidge and Sub-agency structures are Fish Ladders. In addition to a Fish Ladder, a Fish Screen structure was also designed and constructed on Ray Canal. The fish passage will mitigate the loss of hundreds of thousands of fish to the irrigation system. The fish passage project was a combined effort among the Tribes, the US Fish and Wildlife Service, the Bureau of Indian Affairs, Trout Unlimited and the State of Wyoming.

The total cost of these 15 structures (Phase I of the Wind River Irrigation Rehabilitation Project) was $7,713,695.

Without the efforts of the Eastern Shoshone and Northern Arapaho Tribes through the Wind River Water Resource Control Board, Phase I of the rehabilitation process would not be occurring.

The Tribes and WRWRCB continue to pursue additional funds for the rehabilitation effort from the State of Wyoming through the WWDC. The Tribes have come to the table with $730,000 and have requested a matching grant in the amount of $1,482,121 from the Wyoming Water Development Commission. These funds will enable the Tribes to address the rehabilitation of structures identified on the Phase II priority list in Table 1.

Table 1

Wind River Irrigation Project Phase II Priority List

Ranking	Project Name	Total Cost in 2008 Dollars
1	Coolidge Canal Lateral 14B	$254,000
2	Dinwoody Diversion Structure	$552,000
3	Sub-agency Lateral 38 A	$180,000
4	Ray Canal Lateral 37 C System	$432,000
5	Coolidge Canal System	$150,000
6	Sub Agency Canal System	$282,000
7	North Fork Diversion Structure	$300,000
8	Mill Creek / 14B-44 System	$180,000
Total Cost		$2,334,000
	Estimated Cost in 2014 Dollars	$2,583,738
	As per the Bureau of Labor and Statistics Calculator	
Current Funding		
	Tribal Funding	$730,000
	Wyoming Water Development	$1,482,121
Total Funding		$2,212,121

The Tribes will continue this phased approach to the Rehabilitation Process. Additional phases and priority lists will be developed and added as funding is acquired.

Although the Tribes appreciate the financial support of the State of Wyoming, the funding only scratches the surface of what is necessary to bring the Wind River Irrigation Project up to the standards of non-Indian irrigation projects in close proximity to the Wind River Indian Reservation. The Tribes request the aid and assistance of both Senators Barrasso and Enzi and the Senate Committee on Indian Affairs to help secure future funding for the ongoing rehabilitation of the Wind River Irrigation System. For this reason, the Eastern Shoshone and Northern Arapaho Tribes, the Wind River Water Resource Control Board and the Office of the Tribal Water Engineer again endorse S. 438, the "Irrigation Rehabilitation and Renovation for Indian Tribal Governments and Their Economies Act" or the "IRRIGATE Act".

According to the GAO Report 06-314 dated February 2006, the Wind River Irrigation Project was authorized for construction in 1905 but construction was never completed.

The Wind River Irrigation Project is comprised of 3 storage facilities, 11 canals and 377 miles of canals and laterals. These facilities provide water to 38,300 acres of which 67 percent is Indian owned and 33 percent non-Indian owned.

According to the 1994 Natural Resource Consulting Engineers (NRCE) Project Assessment and Plan, no Project-wide rehabilitation of the delivery system has occurred since the 1930's. According to that study due to deferred maintenance over many years, 60 percent or 1200 structures were in need of repair or replacement and 45 percent or 190 miles of canals and laterals need repair or reconstruction. According to the study structure failures were routine resulting in the progressive loss of control of Project water and that catastrophic failure of segments of the delivery system was imminent. According to the 1994 NRCE Project Assessment and Plan due to the Project's current configuration, it only has 66 acres of irrigated land per mile of canal. In comparison, Midvale Irrigation District has over 160 acres per mile of canal. As a general guideline, the Bureau of Reclamation suggests that irrigation projects, in the region, need at least 140 acres of irrigated land per mile of canal to be economically self-sufficient. The study also stated that the resulting poor delivery performance had contributed to a progressive deterioration in crop quality and the water users' ability to pay assessments. It is apparent that the Wind River Irrigation System cannot be considered self-sufficient.

The condition of the Wind River Irrigation Project sadly continues to deteriorate. With the exception of the Tribes' Phase I Rehabilitation Project, little has changed since the 1994 NRCE Wind River Irrigation Project Assessment, the 2006 GAO-Report numbered 06–314 or the 2008 HKM Wind River Irrigation Project Engineering Evaluation and Condition Assessment. The $7,713,695 of Phase I barely scratched the surface in addressing the needs as outlined in the 2008 HKM Wind River Irrigation Project Engineering Evaluation and Condition assessment where the estimated costs for needed replacement construction to be $69,640,000. According to the calculator on the Bureau of Labor and Statistics, something that cost $100 in 2008 cost $110.70 in 2014, which is a 10.7 percent increase; inflation raises those cost to approximately $77,091,500 in 2014.

Clearly something needs to be done. If funds are not made available to deal with the rehabilitation needed, the project will continue to lose water, and both the Indian and non-Indian people who rely on the project, as well as the fisheries impacted by the project, will all suffer.

In addition to the rehabilitation effort, in 2014 the Tribes successfully submitted Level II Phase II Storage Site Study applications to the WWDC. These studies will identify at least 2 suitable storage sites on each of the Big and Little Wind Rivers. The need for additional storage on the Wind River Reservation has been graphically demonstrated during drought years when irrigators have been shut off early in the summer months as early as the first or second week in July. These storage studies and the successful identification of storage sites will not only benefit Tribal irrigators but also all water users on the Wind/Big Horn River system.

What follows is a report on the Wind River Irrigation Rehabilitation Project. The photos graphically show what progress looks like, i.e., what we can jointly accomplish when we have the funding as well as demonstrate what happens when maintenance is deferred and the project is allowed to deteriorate.

In order for the rehabilitation effort to move forward, it will take a united effort from the Eastern Shoshone and Northern Arapaho Tribes, the Bureau of Indian Affairs, the Wyoming Water Development Commission, and our State and Federal Legislators.

Chairman Barrasso, Vice-Chairman Tester and members of the committee, the funding from this bill is simply vital to our efforts. We realize that only through our efforts, and yours, will this absolutely essential rehabilitation occur. Not only can we do this, we must do this.

Chairman Barrasso, the Eastern Shoshone and Northern Arapaho Tribes, the Wind River Water Resource Control Board and the Office of the Tribal Water Engineer strongly endorse S. 438, the "Irrigation Rehabilitation and Renovation for Indian Tribal Governments and Their Economies Act" or the "IRRIGATE Act" as we did S. 715 when the Barrasso amendment was added to it in the previous Congress.

We also encourage members of this committee to do all that is their power to help in moving the IRRIGATE Act forward successfully. The Eastern Shoshone and Northern Arapaho Tribes look forward to working closely with you now and in the future.

Your strong support of the Tribes and their efforts is of the utmost importance. Our efforts will bring much needed relief to both Tribal and non-Tribal irrigators on the Wind River Reservation.

Thank you for your time and consideration.

Attachment

WIND RIVER IRRIGATION REHAB UPDATE

By

THE OFFICE OF THE TRIBAL WATER ENGINEER

The Wind River Water Resource Control Board and the Office of the Tribal Water Engineer appreciates this opportunity to up-date the members of the United States Senate Committee on Indian Affairs on the progress of the Wind River Irrigation Rehabilitation Project.

In 2004 the Wyoming State Legislature appropriated $3,500,000 thru the Wyoming Water Development Commission to assist in the rehabilitation of the Wind River Irrigation Project. These funds were matched with two Federal appropriations in 2006 and 2007 totaling $3,722,500. The combined funding was utilized to rehabilitate irrigation structures in critical need of repair. To this date the total estimated cost of rehabilitating the Irrigation Project remains in the $90M range.

Ray Canal Diversion Structure and Fish Passage

During the 2010- 2011 and 2011-2012 construction seasons the following rehabilitation project structures were completed:

- Coolidge – Trout Creek Diversion Structure
- Johnstown Diversion Structure
- Lefthand Ditch Diversion and Waste Way Structures
- Ray Canal – Mill Creek Crossing Structure

- Ray Canal Diversion Structure
- Coolidge Canal Diversion Structure
- Ray Canal Fish Screen Structure
- Structures: 39-C, 11-C, 59-C, and 14-B

Total cost of rehabilitating these structures was $5,097,095.

In addition to replacing the Ray and Coolidge Canal diversion structures, fish ladders were installed on both diversion structures to enable aquatic life to migrate the stream above and below the diversion structures. A fish screen structure was also constructed in the Ray Canal down steam of the diversion structure. The fish screen will prevent the loss of thousands of fish to the Ray Canal irrigation system. The fish screen structure was built thru the collaborative efforts of various agencies. Funding partners for the fish passage and screens were: USF&W, Trout Unlimited, the Wyoming Wild Life Trust Fund, BIA Wildlife Resources Branch, the WWDC and the Eastern Shoshone and Northern Arapaho Tribes. These funding partners contributed an additional $720,760.

The 2013- 2014 construction season brought this phase of the Wind River Irrigation Rehabilitation Project to a close. WWDC and Federal Funding have been depleted with the start of the 2014 irrigation season. Projects constructed during this period were:

- North Fork Chute
- Willow Creek Diversion Structure
- Meadow Creek Diversion Structure
- Sub-agency Diversion Structure

The total construction costs of these structures were $2,616,599.29.

Sub-agency Diversion Structure

Meadow Creek

Willow Creek

North Fork Chute

It should be noted this rehabilitation project has provided an economic boost to Fremont County, the State of Wyoming and the Wind River Indian Reservation. State and local contractors and sub-contractors have been utilized during the construction projects. These contractors include:

- Inberg-Miller Engineers (Riverton, WY)
- Lowham Walsh LLC (Lander)
- Dowl HKM (Lander)
- High Country Construction (Lander)
- 71 Construction (Riverton)
- Reiman Corp. (Cheyenne)

This phase of the Irrigation Rehab Project has barely scratched the surface of the overall needs of the Wind River Irrigation Project. As stated before the estimated cost of total rehabilitation is in the $90M range. The Office of the Tribal Water Engineer has developed a Phase II list of priorities for rehabilitation. This list and a cost estimate was submitted to the WWDC in November of 2014. We are currently awaiting Wyoming Legislative action on our funding application.

What follows are examples of conditions that currently exist on the Wind River Irrigation Project that need to be addressed in the Rehabilitation Effort.

The CHAIRMAN. Thank you so much for your testimony, Mr. Cottenoir.

Our next witness is Mr. Harry LaBonde, Director, Wyoming Water Development Commission, Cheyenne, Wyoming.

STATEMENT OF HARRY C. LABONDE JR., DIRECTOR, WYOMING WATER DEVELOPMENT COMMISSION

Mr. LaBonde. Chairman Barrasso, Vice Chairman Tester and members of the Committee, thank you for this opportunity to appear before you.

The Wyoming Water Department Commission is charged with developing the water resources of Wyoming for the benefit of its citizens. Those citizens certainly include residents of the Wind River Indian Reservation.

My agency is basically a funding agency where we fund water projects across the State. They tend to fall into two basic categories: potable water systems and irrigation systems. Eligible entities include cities, towns, water districts, irrigation districts and the Northern Arapaho Tribe and the Eastern Shoshone Tribe in Wyoming.

The program is funded with severance tax revenues directed to my program. We fund our water projects with a grant-loan package. Typically, we will see on projects that have access to Federal funding, like projects on the reservation, we will fund those projects at a 50–50 ratio, 50 percent State funds in the form of a grant and the local entity is required to come up with an additional 50 percent of their share.

Occasionally, those projects will have a different Federal share. It depends on the funding scenario. I have seen projects where the Federal share has been 65 percent with a 35 percent State grant. The point is it is a joint program used to develop projects across the State of Wyoming.

On the Wind River Indian Reservation, we have funded a number of potable water systems for Arapaho, Ethete and the Boulder Flats Project developing potable water. We have also funded, as mentioned by Mitch, an irrigation rehabilitation system. That was a 50–50 grant funding scenario. In fact, you see a project for one of the completed diversion structures on that project.

We also have a project coming forward, the next phase, a $2.2 million project and we are funding that project at a 67 percent share grant from the State of Wyoming and a 33 percent share from the local tribes. That was because they did not have access to Federal funds in developing their local share.

In 2008, the BIA commissioned a study for irrigation system assessment on the reservation. They looked at seven or eight irrigation projects, canals that had been developed over the years and generated a cost estimate to repair, replace and upgrade those systems that totaled about $104 million, just on the Wind River Indian Reservation. The $7 million project that has been mentioned was working against that backlog.

If you take that 2008 cost estimate, I just inflated it at 3 percent a year and subtracted the $7 million project, as well as our newer $2 million project, I am still coming up with just short of $120 million of improvements needed on the Wind River Indian Reservation.

One of the obstacles that the tribes face in Wyoming is developing this local funding share. The Wyoming legislature has created a Select Committee on Tribal Relations. I frequently attend their meetings during the year.

One of the expressed concerns at these meetings from tribal irrigators is the inability to get water through their systems, whether it is head gate issues or maintenance issues, they just can't get the water when they need it during the summer months.

That inability to get water and also I will tell you our experience in my program with lining open canals is that it removes seepage or reduces seepage and we see upwards of 30 percent more water being delivered to fields as a result of that.

In terms of this project and developing the local share of funding, it is important for Wyoming to be able to match those funds. We have had to curtail or reduce projects in size because there is not a local share available to match our State funds.

We certainly encourage you to support this bill. I can tell you that when irrigators cannot get their water in the spring or the summer months, their crops do not flourish and as a result, there is a significant impact on the reservation.

I would stand for questions, Mr. Chairman.

[The prepared statement of Mr. LaBonde follows:]

PREPARED STATEMENT OF HARRY C. LABONDE JR., DIRECTOR, WYOMING WATER DEVELOPMENT COMMISSION

Introduction:

Chairman Barrasso, Vice Chairman Tester, and Members of the Committee, my name is Harry C. LaBonde Jr., I serve as director of the Wyoming Water Development Office (WWDO). The mission of the office and its oversight commission, the Wyoming Water Development Commission (WWDC), is to develop Wyoming's water resources for the benefit of the people of the State of Wyoming.

Wyoming Water Development Program

The WWDC is charged with funding a wide variety of water development, infrastructure, renovation, rehabilitation, and conservation projects in the state. Eligible funding entities include cities, towns, water districts, conservation districts, and the Eastern Shoshone and Northern Arapaho Indian Tribes located on the Wind River Indian Reservation (WRIR). Typical projects include:

- Transmission pipelines
- Potable water storage tanks
- Water wells
- Water pump stations
- Irrigation canal rehabilitation
- Irrigation canal structure replacement
- Diversion structure replacement
- Dam and reservoir enlargements
- New dams and reservoirs

Funding for Wyoming's Water Development Program is derived from the collection of severance taxes levied against minerals, oil, and gas resources. Those funds directed to the WWDC are managed in three separate accounts, each having a defined purpose. A brief description of each account follows:

- Water Development Account I – funds new development projects which will develop and use additional Wyoming water resources. Potable water providers have used this fund to expand their systems.
- Water Development Account II – funds the rehabilitation and renovation of existing water systems. Entities responsible for operating irrigation systems have used this fund extensively to upgrade their delivery systems.
- Water Development Account III – funds the planning, design, and construction of new reservoirs in excess of 2000 acre-feet (AF) and reservoir enlargements in excess of 1000 AF.

The Wyoming Water Development Program funds eligible projects with a grant/loan financial package. Typical grants are made at a 67% share with the sponsoring entity responsible for the remaining 33% local share. The local share may be funded by a WWDC loan, which currently carries a 4.0% interest rate. For projects where the sponsor has secured federal funding, a state/federal cost sharing program is implemented. In these situations the typical WWDC grant will vary from 35% or 50% and the federal share varies from 65% to 50%.

Over the years the WWDC has funded, and completed a number of successful projects on the WRIR. Additionally, there are a number of projects in planning, design or under construction. These projects have included both potable water system improvements and irrigation system rehabilitation. Examples include:

- Arapaho Pipeline and Tank *(on-going)*
  - Northern Arapaho Tribe
  - 67% WWDC grant
  - Project Budget = $2,876,000

- Arapaho Water Supply
  - Northern Arapaho Tribe
  - 67% WWDC grant
  - Project budget = $500,000

- Ethete Water Supply *(on-going)*
  - Northern Arapaho Tribe
  - 50% WWDC grant
  - Project Budget = $4,000,000

- Wind River Irrigation
  - Joint Business Council for the Eastern Shoshone and Northern Arapaho Tribes
  - 50% WWDC grant
  - Project Budget = $7,000,000

- Wind River Irrigation Rehabilitation 2015 *(funding approved)*
  - o Eastern Shoshone and Northern Arapaho Tribes
  - o 67% WWDC grant
  - o Project Budget = $2,212,121

- Shoshone Well and Transmission
  - o Eastern Shoshone Tribe
  - o 67% WWDC grant
  - o Project Budget = $1,100,000

- Eastern Shoshone Boulder Flats Well Field
  - o Eastern Shoshone Tribe
  - o 67% WWDC grant
  - o Project Budget = $1,200,000

Through these projects, the WWDC and the two Tribes have developed a positive and successful working relationship which will continue forward on future projects.

Irrigation System Assessment Report
In July 2008, HKM Engineering completed a report titled, "Engineering Evaluation and Condition Assessment Wind River Irrigation Project." This report was commissioned by the Bureau of Indian Affairs and provided a comprehensive assessment of the irrigation systems that serve tribal lands on the WRIR. This included reviews of the following irrigation canals:

- North Fork
- Ray
- Coolidge
- Sub Agency
- Left Hand
- Johnstown
- Upper Wind River

The assessment included a detailed inspection of structures, flumes, siphons, headgates, turnouts, canal banks, and identified canals with high seepage losses. The engineer then prepared cost estimates to correct/replace noted deficiencies, (see attached Table 5 from the report). The combined cost for remediation and replacement totaled $104,452,884 in 2008. Using a 3% annual inflation rate and reducing the cost estimate to account for the two WWDC funded rehabilitation projects, the estimated 2015 cost for irrigation system rehabilitation needs on the WRIR is $119,250,000.

Summary
Irrigation systems on the WRIR are in need of significant rehabilitation and upgrades. Portions of these systems are nearing 100 years of age and reliability of water deliveries has been compromised due to the aging infrastructure. Tribal irrigators depend on

these water deliveries to sustain their farming practices and unreliable irrigation supplies negatively impact the economy of the WRIR.

As noted in the 2008 engineering study, a number of WRIR canals suffer from excessive seepage. Lining of these canals can result in upwards of 30% more water reaching the intended crops, thereby increasing crop outputs and the agricultural economy on the WRIR. The WWDC has funded numerous canal lining or piping projects around the state and the WRIR contains numerous opportunities to continue these types of water conservation projects.

The WWDC has established a good working partnership with both tribes while completing water projects on the WRIR. One of the limiting factors in moving more water projects forward is the lack of available funding for the tribes to meet the sponsor's local share. S.438 provides that much needed funding source and will allow the WRIR tribes to accelerate irrigation rehabilitation projects on the WRIR.

Thank you for the opportunity to testify before the Senate Committee on Indian Affairs.

SUMMARY OF ESTIMATED COSTS FOR NEEDED REMEDIATION

A summary of the estimated costs for remediating the identified deficiencies of the Wind River Irrigation Project irrigation system infrastructure is provided in Table 5. Additionally, the total current replacement value of all Project structures and canal repairs is provided as well.

Table 5 - Summary of Remediation and Replacement Costs

Description	Remediation	Replacement
Structures		
Structure Rehabilitation for Key Canals and Laterals	$6,012,782	$15,407,647
Structure Rehabilitation for Remaining Laterals	$18,004,118	$43,438,536
Subtotal	$24,016,900	$58,846,184
Canals		
Cleaning/Reshaping	$5,306,115	$5,306,115
Seepage Area Lining	$5,488,785	$5,488,785
Subtotal	$10,794,900	$10,794,900
Grand Total	$34,811,800	$69,641,084

\# 104,452,884

The CHAIRMAN. Thank you very much, Mr. LaBonde.
Senator Daines.
Senator DAINES. Thank you, Mr. Chairman.
Before we get started, I want to give a special warm welcome to a group of students from Hardin, Montana, from the Crow and Northern Cheyenne Tribes as well. It is good to have you here watching your government in action. Thanks for being here.
I have a question for Councilman Headdress. Again, it is great to have you here and to have Montana represented so strongly, here on the dais as well as in the crowd. Thanks for taking the time to come here.

I am proud to be a co-sponsor of the IRRIGATE Act. I want to express my support additionally for funding rural water projects at Fort Peck, at Rocky Boy and other BOR projects in addition to the projects included in this bill.

I look forward to working with my colleagues on this Committee to move forward on these important projects for Indian country and for the State of Montana.

Councilman Headdress, I was struck by a comment you made in your testimony. You mentioned the total backlog of deferred maintenance on the Fort Peck irrigation system is $12.7 million.

Mr. HEADDRESS. Yes, sir.

Senator DAINES. How quickly do you expect that number to increase if we continue to delay maintaining this project?

Mr. HEADDRESS. Right now, the actual deferred maintenance cost is closer to $16 million. The best estimate we had was from the BIA's 2014 assessment. I would say those costs have increased by at least $4 million.

Senator DAINES. Could you elaborate on the importance of agriculture on the Fort Peck Reservation and where it ranks in terms of industries for your communities?

Mr. HEADDRESS. At the present time, agriculture is the primary industry for both the tribes and many of our members. Even in the years when we have oil and gas, the income from farming and grazing leases is between 30 and 50 percent. Other revenue is in the tribal budget. When oil and gas income is low, agriculture is even more important.

While I cannot say exactly the percentage of families on the reservation supported by agriculture, I think it is fair to say that is likely close to 30 percent of the families.

Senator DAINES. It is Montana's number one industry, a $5 billion industry across our State.

Mr. HEADDRESS. Yes, sir.

Senator DAINES. How would this project benefit the viability of agriculture for the tribes at Fort Peck?

Mr. HEADDRESS. The project would allow us to put our lands to better use and make sure we are able to productively use our farm lands. This will greatly help us to efficiently use our water resources also.

Senator DAINES. Thank you, Councilman Headdress.

Secretary Washburn, as we look to fund these essential projects, we also must be aware that we cannot keep adding to the national debt which is $18 trillion. Today, the CBO came out with their latest projections that we will be at $25–26 trillion over the course of the next ten years, with $5.6 trillion of interest over the next ten years on the debt alone. Those are probably some pretty conservative interest rates.

In your view, what are some ways we can find savings in the BIA budget or the Department of Interior, more generally, to fund these irrigation projects and other high priority items for Indian country?

Mr. WASHBURN. Let me not rate my colleagues in other parts of the Department of Interior. I wouldn't be welcome if I started offering up other peoples' budget.

Senator DAINES. We will welcome you back, that is all right.

Mr. WASHBURN. Thank you.

You raise a really hard question. We have a lot of priorities particularly in Indian affairs, all of which we cannot possibly meet. This is one of the frustrating things we face every day. We don't have all the money we would like to accomplish everything we need to do.

Irrigation projects are not the only place where we have a backlog in deferred maintenance, schools, detention centers and other areas. That is why these things are so difficult.

Indeed, many institutions tend to let go of long term maintenance type stuff to save money so they can do other things. Whenever budgets get tight, that is one of the first things people turn to, let us stop taking care of the stuff we have now and doing routine maintenance.

That is a little bit of how we got here. There are some other complications to that but it is not easy to find the funds to pay these sorts of things. If the Administration has concerns, it is largely around those. How do we pay for this?

Senator DAINES. The concern is the continuing delays. The price for maintenance keeps going up and we are losing economic growth opportunities which create more taxes and so forth and for our people in Montana.

Can I get your commitment that we can work together to find the necessary savings? It is never easy, the budget process. I understand that but I think we can work to prioritize some of these essential items like these irrigation projects.

I don't want to keep introducing bills over and over and we come back and recycle the same testimony. Let us figure out a way to get it done.

Mr. WASHBURN. We are happy to work with you, Senator, and with the leadership of the Committee.

Senator DAINES. I appreciate it. Thank you.

The CHAIRMAN. Thank you, Senator Daines.

Senator Tester?

Senator TESTER. Thank you, Mr. Chairman.

I have a few questions for Charles too. It is good to have you here.

Do you know offhand how many acres are under irrigation at Fort Peck now?

Mr. HEADDRESS. I am not sure on that. I will have to find out.

Senator TESTER. If we pass this IRRIGATE Act, would you be able to add additional acres under your irrigation?

Mr. HEADDRESS. Yes, we would, Senator Tester. We have projects for which we have plans. The bench above Sprole is a good potential spot to plant crops like potatoes, certain types of potatoes. If we have an irrigation project in that area or coming up to it, that would be a great boon to our economy.

Senator TESTER. Let me ask you the same question a little differently. Do you have land right now that was irrigated say 15, 20 or 25 years ago that now the system no longer can support?

Mr. HEADDRESS. Again, I will have to defer that to our experts. I am not sure about that but I will find out for you.

Senator TESTER. That would be great.

Offhand, do you have any tribal members this would impact if we were to get this passed?

Mr. HEADDRESS. If were to get this passed? Could you rephrase that question?

Senator TESTER. How many members of your tribe would be impacted by a good irrigation system that would work well?

Mr. HEADDRESS. At least 8,000, sir.

Senator TESTER. You mentioned the department has charged some of the irrigation system users to repay construction costs, user fees. What impact has that has on the tribe or individual landowners and what would forgiving that debt on the Fort Peck tribes do to help drive this project forward?

Mr. HEADDRESS. The debt is a problem for both our members and the tribes. I can speak from personal experience. My son inherited a fractional interest in trust land sold by the irrigation project.

As soon as he inherited this land, he was hounded by aggressive and threatening demand letters saying he had to pay the outstanding debt on the project, not on the whole project, of course.

My son is trying to make the payments but when he inherited this land, he had no idea he was inheriting a debt. This land is lying idle. It is not being irrigated and in production, yet he has to pay this levy.

The debt is also a problem for the tribes. We are trying to repurchase a fractionated interest through the Land Buyback Program. In order to do this, the tribes have been told that we also have to pay the past debt on these lands.

Forgiving the debt would make a major difference. You might recall the claims in the Keepseagle case when non-Indians were getting debt forgiveness but Indians were not. Many of those neighbors who had debt forgiven got a new chance and are in successful business today.

Senator TESTER. Thank you, Charles. Again, thanks for making the trek from Montana. We appreciate your testimony.

Mr. HEADDRESS. It is good to see you. Thank you.

Senator TESTER. Kevin, the bill we are talking about, S. 438, will benefit Indian irrigation systems by creating a dedicated stream of funding for these projects from the Reclamation Fund. As I said in my opening comments, the IRRIGATE Act originated from a larger bill that used the Reclamation Fund also to pay for Indian water rights and rural water projects.

Can you describe the effect of not having a dedicated stream of funding on delaying implementation of these water settlements and rural water projects, as well as the impact on deferred maintenance on these projects?

Mr. WASHBURN. Yes, Senator Tester, I can. What happens is we have to ask you for the money every year and hope and pray that we get it. That is sort of the way it goes. We do these long term water rights settlements and we commit to long term amounts of money. If that money doesn't come through, then the water rights settlements sometimes falls through.

It is important for us to have some certainty. We have a lot of water rights settlements that we have already committed to. Frankly, we have a lot of water rights settlements in the process that we hope to commit to in the future.

I will tell you that the drought is affecting us all over the west. Drought is serious. I saw an article a couple days ago saying the war in Syria was partially responsible for drought. We are glad that we are in a country that doesn't go to war about these sorts of things but they are very serious matters and raise the stakes of these kinds of issues.

Senator TESTER. There is no doubt about that. If we were going to finish all the water projects out there right now, water settlement projects, how many dollars would that be?

Mr. WASHBURN. I can provide that to you. It is in the hundreds of millions.

Senator TESTER. It is in the hundreds of millions. I wouldn't expect you to know this but there is $30 million in the Bureau of Reclamation Fund in this budget to take care of those water projects.

I am saying if we are going to move forward on this stuff, it is going to take Congress to act to appropriate some money to do it, to be quite frank with you, because we are talking about hundreds of millions of dollars, maybe even $1 billion.

I appreciate the work you have done and the hard decisions you have had to make already. There is more to do and I have a few more questions around.

Thanks, Mr. Chairman.

The CHAIRMAN. Senator Cantwell?

STATEMENT OF HON. MARIA CANTWELL,
U.S. SENATOR FROM WASHINGTON

Senator CANTWELL. Thank you, Mr. Chairman. Thank you for holding this important hearing.

I too want to ask Assistant Secretary Washburn a question. Thank you for being here.

I want to ask about the Wapato Project which is on the Yakama Nation in central Washington. It is one of the more troubled irrigation systems run by the Bureau of Indian Affairs.

According to the GAO study, there is more than $130 million in delayed maintenance for that project. Yet, the Wapato Project is for area farmers, tribal members. It has been in operation for more than 100 years providing for 150,000 acres on the Yakama Reservation.

Some of the water deliveries were halted in the summer causing acute economic hardship for many farmers.

Last year, we had Ruth Jim, who serves on the Yakama Nation Tribal Council to testify before the Committee. Councilman Jim reported that the supplies of water are increasingly unreliable. Part of the problem is leaky and unlined delivery canals, less reliability over time, and lack of reliable irrigated water is harming fish recovery efforts. We are all focused on the efforts for fish recovery.

I feel the Bureau is being derelict on our trust responsibilities to the tribes. What do you think we need to do to get this problem addressed now before it gets worse?

Mr. WASHBURN. We have a bunch of hardworking folks in our irrigation offices at the Bureau. We have something like 400 employees who work on this every day and care a lot about it.

I guess I won't own the fact that the BIA alone has been derelict; we have all contributed to that. Certainly Congress has too. Chairman Barrasso explained this most clearly in a previous hearing when he said these projects were supposed to be self sustaining and they never were, honestly. That started well over 100 years ago. He called it the gap between the theory and the reality. It actually is something that has added up over time.

In 2006, GAO said we weren't assessing enough money for the users of these systems. We have increased the assessments, particularly at Wapato, for example. We think we have probably rightsized the assessments, that if everything was up to snuff, the assessments would be fine going forward to cover O&M.

The problem is it doesn't pay for 100 years or at least many decades of under-funding of those costs. It took us a long time to get into this mess and it is not something that we will quickly get out of. We need to work on that.

Senator CANTWELL. What are the next steps to address the problem?

Mr. WASHBURN. The President has added $1.5 million to this year's budget request. That raises our budget request from I think $12.3 million to the $11–$12 million range. It is not a lot of money but it is a start.

Senator CANTWELL. Will some of that money be spent on this particular irrigation repair?

Mr. WASHBURN. Some of it is for irrigation O&M generally, so yes, I would assume a portion of that would go towards Wapato. We don't have that many irrigation projects. That is both a blessing and a curse because it means there is not wide support across Indian country for correcting these problems. There is only a handful of tribes that really benefit, so that is a challenge for us.

It is a challenge we definitely need to meet better than we have been doing.

Senator CANTWELL. I am glad to hear that some of the resources would go to Wapato and certainly want to look at addressing shortfall in the future.

Mr. WASHBURN. Thank you.

Senator CANTWELL. Thank you, Mr. Chairman.

The CHAIRMAN. Thank you very much.

Senator Daines, any additional questions?

Senator DAINES. No.

The CHAIRMAN. Secretary Washburn, your written testimony recommends adding personnel to the list of deferred maintenance items authorized by this bill. To me, this bill is intended to cover repairing structures, not actually increasing administrative expenses.

Some water users have raised concerns with this Committee that their fees are used more for administrative costs than for actual maintenance. Can you elaborate a bit on the need for the additional personnel you are recommending?

Mr. WASHBURN. When those ditches are clogged with weeds, it is human beings that go and pull those weeds. You have to have personnel to do that work. That is basically the bottom line.

There are lots of other examples like that but maintaining all these structures requires human beings. I guess that is why I would say personnel are important. Personnel are key. We have a lot of hardworking people here but obviously we don't have enough of them to do the job.

The CHAIRMAN. Once the bill is enacted, the Bureau is going to need to be ready to timely undertake construction and maintenance repairs. There are other Federal agencies that manage large water infrastructure projects such as the Bureau of Reclamation.

Has the Bureau examined and adopted best practices used by other agencies so that it is ready to go for these additional responsibilities?

Mr. WASHBURN. The bill was only recently introduced, so I am not sure we have every plan in place that we need. I will tell you if you gave me $770 million today, which is what this bill projects, I would not be able to spend $770 million in a responsible way.

However, over time we can. If this bill was enacted, we would definitely endeavor to spend that money in an appropriate way and put it to good work.

The CHAIRMAN. Ms. Fennell, nine years have passed since the GAO issued its report highlighting the shortcomings of Indian irrigation systems. The report concluded the Bureau did not know to what extent its irrigation projects were capable of financially sustaining themselves.

For example, the Bureau did not know how much it would cost to financially sustain each specific irrigation project.

How could the study by the BIA required by this bill address the financial sustainability issues raised by your GAO report?

Ms. FENNELL. The study that is contained in the bill appears to be looking at the programmatic issues of BIA. We think that there might be some opportunities for clarification in the bill as to whether funds could be utilized for conducting the financial sustainability assessments that we recommended in our report.

We would be very happy to work with your staff in terms of any clarification on that.

The CHAIRMAN. Thank you.

Mr. Cottenoir, in some locations, the Wind River irrigation infrastructure is dilapidated, in my opinion, beyond use. You would have a better idea than I, but that is certainly the report I have had.

What is the efficiency, in your mind, of the Wind River Irrigation Project, the whole project?

Mr. COTTENOIR. I visited with the Bureau of Indian Affairs folks and the actual efficiency has not been quantified. They base it on similar irrigation projects with similar canals, evaporation rate, canal losses and structure losses.

The estimated efficiency is somewhere between 35 to 45 percent.

The CHAIRMAN. Is a number that low sustainable, thinking about the impact to the system and the users of what seems to me like a low efficiency rate?

Mr. COTTENOIR. It is a very low efficiency rate. Right now, if nothing is done, that efficiency rate cannot be sustained. It can only be decreased. With increased funding and rehabilitation of the system, those efficiency rates could be raised.

With the current state of affairs and the current maintenance and schedule that BIA has, I don't think even that 35 percent efficiency rate could be sustained. I think you would see that decreasing as time goes on.

The CHAIRMAN. Users pay an annual assessment to operate the system and it is only working at 35 percent. Do all users pay or only those individuals who receive water a lot must pay?

Mr. COTTENOIR. Everybody that has a water right on the reservation pays an assessment. They are charged the assessment even though, in some cases, there is an inability to deliver water. For some reason, the allottee cannot lease their lands. Because of the increasing O&M rate, it makes it not viable for an allottee to lease their lands, so that goes unpaid.

Yes, everybody is assessed that O&M fee, whether they receive water or not.

The CHAIRMAN. They end up having to pay, even if they don't get any water. If they are not getting any water or if they cannot afford to irrigate their land and don't pay the fees, what happens to those folks?

Mr. COTTENOIR. In many cases, that O&M rate, the assessment rate, accrues over time. Certain individuals are turned over to Treasury. In some cases, many of our elderly people and allottees are turned over to Treasury and in many cases, their social security is attached. It just continues to spiral out of control.

The CHAIRMAN. Let me get this clear. They are not actually receiving any water because the system itself is dilapidated and only working at 35–40 percent. They are not getting any water; they are still required to pay and if they don't pay, they are turned over to the Treasury Department for collections or garnishing of some of the payments that are due to them. Is that an accurate assessment of what you are seeing at home?

Mr. COTTENOIR. Yes, Senator Barrasso. In many cases, that is the case. I also stated in many cases, the increasing on them just makes it not viable for them to lease their land. If they don't lease their land, they cannot pay the O&M.

The CHAIRMAN. I have one last question, Mr. Cottenoir. In addition to the efforts of the Wyoming State and the tribal governments to address the irrigation problems, the two tribes on the reservation are also encouraging users to perhaps form a water association or water associations.

How would this bill empower the tribes or the local water user associations to improve the Indian irrigation system?

Mr. COTTENOIR. Forming the water association throws the responsibility to operate and maintain onto the actual water users who know what they need and how to do it. If the money comes to the tribes and we continue to form these associations, if we do 638, the program, then it would be our responsibility to take care of that.

We are the ones who know how to do it. We are the ones who have proven we have the ability to do that along with our partnership we formed with the Wyoming Water Development Commission and the State of Wyoming.

The CHAIRMAN. Thank you, Mr. Cottenoir.

Mr. LaBonde, I will get to you in a couple seconds. I wanted to go to a second round first. Senator Tester.

Senator TESTER. Thank you, Mr. Chairman.

We are going to go back to you, Kevin. Nobody knows trust responsibility better than you. I mean that with the highest regard. We have heard about the department imposing fees and construction repayments on Indian irrigation system uses. Can you talk about whether or not these fees are appropriate for tribal trust lands?

Mr. WASHBURN. I think absolutely. We certainly have to charge all the users on the system to the extent it is appropriate to do so. I think our highest responsibility for these systems—this work isn't formed by the trust responsibilities and that is our highest responsibility, but some of them do charge the Indian lands. I think they won't work unless we assess some of the tribal lands as well.

To make these things work economically, we have to do that. Again, many of these were supposed to be self-sustaining when originally envisioned. Our policies have changed dramatically towards Indian tribes and Indian people since these things were first authorized.

We have to go with the assumptions that were underway when they were authorized, which was that they ultimately be self-sustaining. We have to charge the users, whether they are non-Indian irrigators or Indian and tribal irrigators.

Senator TESTER. These dollars would stay in that reservation or moved to different reservations?

Mr. WASHBURN. They generally stay in that reservation. They get assessed and they go to the Treasury, but they get directed back to that reservation for operation and maintenance of the system.

Senator TESTER. As a matter of fact, are there administrative fees cut off those dollars when they flow to the Treasury and then back?

Mr. WASHBURN. You mean does the Treasury take a cut or something like that?

Senator TESTER. Or does your department take a cut?

Mr. WASHBURN. I don't know but we can certainly get you that information.

Senator TESTER. Okay.

I have a question for Harry. Can you describe the condition of the Wind River irrigation system, I hope you haven't asked this already, Mr. Chairman, relative to other irrigation systems in Wyoming? Can you describe the condition of Wind River versus other irrigation systems?

Mr. LABONDE. Senator Tester, it is one of the systems in poorer condition across the State of Wyoming. With other districts, I see active programs to upgrade the system. My agency assists with that but they are assessing the irrigators for a portion of those costs.

Senator TESTER. I think it is great you have been able to fund the projects at Wind River. There is no doubt about that. I am curious if the Commission considers the Wind River irrigation system at the same level or priority as other irrigation systems in the State when you talk about funding decisions?

Mr. LABONDE. Most definitely. We consider all of those applicants equally. I am not aware that we have turned down an application from the Wind River Indian Reservation.

Senator TESTER. I am going back to you, Secretary Washburn. The bill, as drafted, creates authorization for the department to take money from reclamation funds each year and apply those funds to irrigation projects.

Correct me if I am wrong, but funding maintenance for those irrigation systems is currently authorized, is that correct?

Mr. WASHBURN. Yes, Senator. There certainly are authorizations in place.

Senator TESTER. That is the right answer.

Mr. WASHBURN. It is about appropriations.

Senator TESTER. That is my next question. As we move forward on this bill, would we have to make this funding mandatory to make sure the IRRIGATE Act is effective?

Mr. WASHBURN. When you start to talk about mandatory funding, that is kind of a term of art in the budget context. I am not sure we, ordinary citizens, intend what mandatory means in that context, sort of the OMB context.

The Administration has asked Congress to provide mandatory funding for contract support costs but that means we don't appropriate it every year. It comes out of the mandatory side of the budget.

No, I don't think you have to make this funding mandatory to make it happen, but we would need some sort of assured source of funding to make it happen.

Senator TESTER. I want to thank everyone who testified today. I very much appreciate your testimony. I think this is a real important issue for Indian country. Moving forward, hopefully we can come up with some solutions and get some problems solved.

Thank you all.

The CHAIRMAN. Thank you, Senator Tester.

Senator Cantwell?

Senator CANTWELL. Thank you, Mr. Chairman.

I wanted to follow up with Ms. Fennell because obviously we have the Act before us but do you think there are other things we need to do to tackle this problem? Do you think there are administrative things within the way the projects are prioritized or administered?

Ms. FENNELL. The Senate bill that is before us could help address a number of the issues we raised in our 2006 report. We have not had an opportunity to further evaluate the state of the irrigation projects since 2006. We stand ready to assist the Committee with any additional work that may be needed.

There are probably some longer term issues that would be important to address going forward in terms of looking at these irrigation projects, some of which date back to the late 1800s or early 1900s, and to think about whether or not there are questions about modernizing these projects given the scarcity of water and the advanced technologies that currently exist.

In terms of the bill itself, we do think it would largely address a lot of the issues we did raise back in 2006.

Senator CANTWELL. Did you discuss anything about climate change impacts on water in your report?

Ms. FENNELL. Not specifically in that report. We did visit 9 of the 16 projects. We identified the types of issues we saw and the state of the projects at that time. We have not followed up since that particular time.

Senator CANTWELL. Thank you, Mr. Chairman.

The CHAIRMAN. Thank you, Senator Cantwell.

Mr. LaBonde, thank you for being here and testifying. A number of the comments you made fit completely with what I heard as well when we had field hearings in 2011.

Your written testimony describes numerous projects you have worked on with the tribes on the reservation. State contributions have assisted in improving portions of the irrigation systems.

Your testimony further noted there is great need for significant rehabilitation and upgrade. How big of an impact would rehabilitation and upgrade really have on the Wind River area and local communities, if it were completed, in terms of the economy, economic opportunities, jobs and those sorts of things?

Mr. LABONDE. The Wind River Indian Reservation I would characterize as an agricultural operation raising grass, hay and alfalfa hay to support ranching operations. If the water is not available or if the water is in the creek or the rivers and you cannot get it down the ditch, basically you don't have a hay crop. That has a significant impact.

I don't have any figures to offer to you but I can say that when ranching operations don't have water, they suffer significantly. As I said earlier in my testimony, I have heard that from Indian irrigators at the Select Tribal Relations Committee meetings.

The CHAIRMAN. Your written testimony noted that a 2008 engineering study found excessive water seepage from the Wind River Irrigation Project. I think you mentioned lining the canals could result in upwards of 30 percent more water reaching the crops.

Senator Tester asked how you would compare the conditions at the Wind River Irrigation Project with neighboring, non-tribal irrigation systems you have seen around the State.

Can you describe for all of us and for the record what sort of differences there are and some of the things you have said, that this is one of the worse systems in terms of the needs?

Mr. LABONDE. Some of the observations I would offer are in terms of the structures, basically concrete structures, you see a picture there of a newer structure. When you look at structures on the reservation, you find significantly deteriorated concrete, even to the point where the structures look like they may fail totally.

With other systems, you see ditch banks or canals that are maintained, weed burning, weed growth, trees that are removed so that water can flow unimpeded. Also in systems around the State that we funded, we are also upgrading the technology so a lot of the control gates are actually operated from a remote site or from the irrigation district's office. That is a labor saving mechanism so that you don't have to dispatch somebody out to adjust a gate.

All of those things were observed in some of the other systems, non-tribal systems.

The CHAIRMAN. Mr. Cottenoir, I don't know if you can do this estimation but I wondered if you could estimate how many acres are currently not being farmed because of the situation and needs, that could be brought back into production if the system was operating efficiently?

We heard from Mr. Headdress you are handling an area of 2 million acres, larger than the size of Rhode Island. I am trying to get it into context.

Mr. COTTENOIR. I don't have an accurate figure for you but we are currently doing a study to assess all the irrigated acres, all the acres that aren't currently being irrigated, and the reason for that. We should have that completed by the end of the year. We should have a very accurate accounting of the exact number of acres out of production because of no water.

The CHAIRMAN. I want to thank all of you. I want to remind the witnesses your full written testimony will be made a part of the official hearing record.

Just to let you know, some of the members who may not have been here today will be submitting written and follow-up questions. The record for this hearing will remain open for two weeks.

I want to thank each and every one of you for your time and your testimony today.

This hearing is adjourned.

[Whereupon, at 3:49 p.m., the Committee was adjourned.]

APPENDIX

PREPARED STATEMENT OF THE COLORADO RIVER INDIAN TRIBES (CRIT)

The Colorado River Indian Tribes (CRIT) greatly appreciates the opportunity to submit this written testimony for the Senate Indian Affairs Committee hearing on Chairman Barrasso's pending legislation, S. 438, Irrigation Rehabilitation and Renovation for Indian Tribal Governments and Their Economies Act.

CRIT appreciates the Chairman's efforts to focus Congressional attention on unaddressed capital finance needs for Indian Country infrastructure. The Federal obligation to resolve the deferred maintenance and replacement needs on the Indian irrigation projects is especially strong. These projects are often the backbone of the economy for rural Indian reservations, which is the case for the Colorado River Indian Reservation.

Nearly a decade ago the General Accounting Office (GAO) presented a stark account of the crippling deferred maintenance backlog at the Colorado River Irrigation Project (CRIP) and the other Bureau of Indian Affairs (BIA) operated irrigation projects. *Indian Irrigation Projects: Numerous Issues Need to Be Addressed to Improve Project Management and Financial Sustainability* (GAO–06–314) (February 2006) ("2006 Report").

CRIT applauds the Committee for securing an updated report from the General Accounting Office (GAO) on whether the BIA is addressing maintenance backlogs at the irrigation projects. *Indian Irrigation Projects: Deferred Maintenance and Financial Sustainability Issues Remain Unresolved* (GAO–15–453–T) (March 4, 2015) ("2015 Report").

The 2015 Report reiterates several key insights on addressing the deferred maintenance backlog and also reaffirms that the overall scale of the deferred maintenance problem on BIA-managed irrigation systems still exceeds $500 million dollars—even using the BIA's own figures.

CRIT recognizes that the GAO has not verified this BIA-supplied information on either an overall or project-by-project basis. CRIT is, nevertheless, astonished and greatly concerned to read in the 2015 Report that the BIA is reporting an "updated" maintenance backlog at CRIP that is an eight-fold decrease from the BIA's previous cost estimate—the CRIP maintenance backlog cost in the 2006 Report is $134,758,664, as compared to a figure of approximately $17,000,000 in the 2015 Report. No major maintenance or repairs have occurred in the intervening years to account for this stunning reduction in cost estimate.

One of the GAO's key recommendations for addressing the deferred maintenance backlog is on the need to base plans for remediation on reliable information. As the GAO explained in the 2006 Report: "Information on financial sustainability, along with accurate deferred maintenance information, are both critical pieces of information needed to have a debate on the long-term direction of BIA's irrigation program. Once this information is available, the Congress and interested parties will be able to address how the deferred maintenance will be funded (and otherwise implemented)."

Contrary to the $17 million figure the BIA reportedly provided to the GAO, the evidence is overwhelming that the BIA's 2006 remediation cost estimate of $134,758,664 reflects the actual price tag for adequate CRIP remediation. (It is important to emphasize that the 2006 figure more closely reflects the correct scale of the cost for addressing the CRIP deferred remediation backlog; CRIT was not provided, and consequently has not reviewed, either the 2006 or 2015 BIA cost estimates.)

The attached document provides an overview of the technical and financial basis for CRIT's conclusion that the cost of addressing the remediation backlog at CRIP is at least several tens of millions of dollars more than the BIA's present estimate, and certainly the cost remains well over $100 million.

CRIT would be pleased to answer any questions and/or provide additional information to the Committee and/or the GAO on this testimony, including the details in the attached Summary and Tables on Colorado River Irrigation Project—Deferred

Remediation Costs. Devin Rhinerson will serve as CRIT's primary point of contact for answering any questions or supplying any additional information requested by the Chairman, Ranking Member, or any other SCIA members.

In closing, CRIT again commends the Chairman for his decision to hold this hearing and for his attention to addressing the critical need for infrastructure investment in Indian Country.

Attachment

Summary Details and Tables on Colorado River Irrigation Project (CRIP)— Deferred Remediation Costs

The GAO has consistently advised Congress that well-managed and adequate irrigation remediation projects require accurate, reliable, and up-to-date information on irrigation project facilities in need of rehabilitation or replacement. Based on this recommendation, the BIA commissioned HKM to conduct an irrigation condition assessment on CRIP, which assessment was completed in 2011. *CRIT Project, Engineering Evaluation and Condition Assessment, CRIP* (April 2011) ("HKM Report").

The HKM Report strongly suggests that the CRIP remediation backlog cost can be addressed for less than $20 million. For example, the HKM Report states that "[a] summary of the estimated cost for remediating the identified deficiencies of the Colorado River Irrigation Project infrastructure is provided in table 5." Table 5 of the HKM Report ("HKM Table 5") is titled "Summary of Remediation and Replacement Costs" and shows a total of $18,451,022 for "rehabilitation."

There are at least three (3) reasons the HKM Table 5 cannot —or, at least should not— be construed as a reliable estimate of the deferred maintenance costs that must be address to complete an adequate CRIP remediation, as follows:

1. HKM Table 5 ($18,451,022) is based almost entirely on estimated costs for rehabilitating facilities while costs based on replacing CRIP features are systematically omitted, even features where the HKM Report indicates a compelling need for replacement.

   a. Anticipated remediation costs and timeframes are rendered inaccurate when facilities that are in need of replacement are incorrectly classified as needing only refurbishing and rehabilitation. For example, the HKM Report indicates that Ramp Flume "1WR9" can be rehabilitated. Nevertheless, photographs in the HKM Report reveal that ¼ to ⅓ of the Ramp Flume is missing, making it highly unlikely that this CRIP feature can be adequately remediated by simply rehabilitating the flume at an estimated cost of $30,338.09. In fact, adequate remediation of the Ramp Flume will require its replacement at four times the cost of the (highly-questionable) rehabilitation cost estimate.

   b. The HKM Report is a budget level study, which is a rough estimate of the cost to perform the described work. The Bureau of Reclamation (BoR) Directives and Standards (FAC 09–01) recommend the use of a contingency factor of twenty percent (20 percent) to twenty-five percent (25 percent) for this level of study. The HKM Report uses a fifteen percent (15 percent) contingency factor for structure rehabilitation cost estimates and 10 percent factor for canal liner rehabilitation.

   c. The cost of replacing the eleven key canal and lateral structures rated by HKM as "CMDM critical and serious" that were in need of replacement, in addition to the two such structures already marked for replacement by HKM, is $8,764,378, based on the replacement cost data from the HKM Report. The total adjusted cost is $9,465,528 after applying the appropriate contingency factor. Cost adjustments are identified in CRIT Table 2 and reflected on Row #1 of CRIT Table 1.

   d. CRIT Table 1 shows that the remediation cost of the items included on HKM Table 5 ($18,451,022) is more accurately a range between $30,064,091 and $61,093,416. The adjusted remediation costs of these items is presented as a range, between $30,064,091 to $61,093,416, because the small sample size used by HKM to develop its rehabilitation/replacement costs for the Structures -Remaining Laterals category in the HKM Report and Canal Liner Rehabilitation creates uncertainty as to whether to use replacement or rehabilitation as the anticipated remediation cost and also for gauging how much of the existing canal lining should be replaced. These estimates are further adjusted by applying the appropriate contingency factor of 25 percent. These adjustments to HKM's cost estimates are reflected on Row #2 of CRIT Table 1.

e. The canal lining remediation cost range based on 10 percent to 25 percent of the cost of replacing some portion of the sections of canal lining rated by HKM as C&ODM serious for canal liner rehabilitation was estimated to be between $5,338,764 and $13,346,908 using cost data from the HKM Report for canal lining replacement. The total adjusted cost range is $12,762,714 to $21,499,599 after applying the appropriate contingency factor. The cost adjustment is shown on Row #4 of CRIT Table 1.

f. Costs were only included in the HKM Report for the safety ladder replacement, but not for installing new safety escape ladders to meet BoR standards. HKM acknowledged that escape ladders were spaced for 750 feet to one-half mile apart and that many of the installed ladders had been destroyed by canal maintenance activities. BoR standards call for escape ladders to be installed at 750-foot intervals on each side of the canal or lateral. Safety ladders are installed on alternating sides of the canal or lateral every 375 feet. Based on BoR standards, 1,046 safety ladders will be required in the currently lined sections of the Project at a cost of $744,235, using the HKM cost data. HKM included $133,097 for escape ladders which, when adjusted for the appropriate contingency factor, is $145,196. The adjustments to estimated costs are shown on Row #6 of CRIT Table 1. An additional $599,039 will be required to meet BoR standards for safety escape ladders. Additional ladders will be required if the remaining unlined key canals and laterals are lined. See Row #8 of CRIT Table 1.

2. There are cost-related factors, such as the cost contingencies and sample size used by HKM that result in inaccurate or at least unreliable cost estimates for items included in HKM Table 5 and also elsewhere in the HKM Report.

3. There are key categories of CRIP facilities that are not included in HKM Table 5, even though these omitted features are identified and also documented in the HKM Report as needing remediation, installation, and/or replacement.

a. No costs were included in the HKM Report for resurfacing operation and maintenance roads. Yet, consistently throughout the Canal Cleaning/Reshaping Reports and Canal Liner Rehabilitation Reports in Appendix F of the HKM Report, HKM recommended the resurfacing of the maintenance roads. If the O&M roads are resurfaced on both sides of the canals and laterals, there will be 276 miles to be resurfaced, based on the lengths of lined and unlined canals and laterals described in the HKM Report. This cost could be significant addition to the total estimated cost of rehabilitation and replacement of system features.

b. The unaddressed cost for resurfacing O&M roads on the Project will be between $8,976,845 and $20,518,502 depending on the widths of the O&M roads and whether one or both sides are resurfaced. CRIT Table 3 shows the cost of resurfacing 14 and 16 feet wide O&M roads on one side of the canals and laterals and both sides.

c. The unaddressed cost for lining the remaining unlined canals and laterals in the Project is $138,334,934 as shown on CRIT Table 3. (The lining of the unlined canals and laterals will take several years to complete because of the need to keep the system in service and line small segments each year.)

The BIA's more recent deferred maintenance cost estimate might be derived, in whole or in part, from the HKM Report. The details summarized above demonstrate the BIA's $17 million cost estimate is incorrect and unreliable, even if it is based on the HKM Report. Addressing the present CRIP remediation backlog will require tens of millions of dollars more that the BIA's present estimate and certainly well over $100 million.

The following tables are attached:

CRIT Table 1. Comparison of Certain HKM-Identified Remediation Items

CRIT Table 2. Structure Remediation Cost Adjustment for Eleven Structures on Key Canals and Laterals

CRIT Table 3. Estimated Cost of Unaddressed Deficiencies

CRIT Table 1. Comparison of Certain HKM-Identified Remediation Items

Row Number	HKM Redacted Report Reference	Feature Description	HKM Rehabilitation Cost, $	CRIT Anticipated Remediation Cost, $	HKM Replacement Cost, $ (1)	Basis/Amount for Remediation Cost Differences
1	Vol. I, Pages 6-8 Vol. II, App. F, pp. F-3 through F-12 and pp. F-28 through F-259	Structures – Key Canals and Laterals	5,354,930	9,465,528	39,112,067	$701,145 reflecting appropriate contingency factor (HKM 15%, CRIT 25%), $8,764,378.
2	Vol. I, Table 3, page 13	Structures – Remaining Laterals	6,101,353	6,589,461 to 28,798,951	26,665,677	$488,108 to $2,133,254 reflecting appropriate contingency factor (HKM 15%, CRIT 25%). CRIT used a remediation cost range of $6,589,461 to $28,798,931.
3	Vol. I, page 15, Vol III, page F-536	Canal Constriction	41,274	41,274	41,274	No change was made to HKM rehabilitation cost because based on present knowledge there was no basis to justify a change.
4	Vol. III, App. F pp. F-350 through F-553	Canal Liner Rehabilitation	6,359,416	12,762,714 to 21,499,599	147,146,063	$1,064,534 to 1,793,275 reflecting appropriate contingency factor (HKM 10%, CRIT 20%). $5,338,764 to 13,346,908.
5	Vol. I, pp. 16-17, Vol. III, App. F, pp. F-315 through F-349	Cleaning/Reshaping	460,952	460,952	460,952	No change was made to HKM rehabilitation cost because based on present knowledge there was no basis to justify a change.
6	Vol. I, page 15, Vol III, App. F, pp. 534-535	Safety Feature Rehabilitation	133,097	145,196	228,166	$12,099 reflecting appropriate contingency factor (HKM 10%, CRIT 20%).
7	Vol. III, App. F, page F-514	Tunnel Rehabilitation	0	0	1,728,730	No change was made to HKM rehabilitation cost because based on present knowledge there was no basis to justify a change.
8	Vol. I, page 15, Vol I, App. D, page D-9	Safety Escape Ladders	0	599,039	0	$599,039 for safety ladders not included by HKM
		Cost Total	18,451,022	30,064,091 to 61,093,416	215,382,929	

(1) HKM included Replacement costs only for comparison, HKM Report, April 2011, Vol. I page iii and page 3.

CRIT Table 2. Structure Remediation Cost Adjustment for Eleven Structures on Key Canals and Laterals

Structure Type	HKM Reference HKM App. F	Rehab Cost Reference HKM App. D	CRV Reference HKM App. D	Deficiency		HKM Remediation Cost Reference HKM App. D	CRIT Revised Remediation Cost (1)	Difference
				Category	Rating			
		$	$			$	$	$
Ramp Flume	Pg.F-249	30,338	139,090	CMDM	Critical	30,338	139,090	108,752
Lateral Headgate	Pg.F-237	108	219,164	CMDM	Critical	108	219,164	219,056
Check (NT)	Pg.F-66	105,350	563,444	CMDM	Serious	105,350	563,444	458,094
Check (NT)	Pg.F-68	102,718	563,444	CMDM	Serious	102,718	563,444	460,726
Check (NT)	Pg.F-67	102,674	566,212	CMDM	Serious	102,674	566,212	463,538
Check (NT)	Pg.F-69	102,674	563,444	CMDM	Serious	102,674	563,444	460,770
Check (NT)	Pg.F-70	102,674	563,444	CMDM	Serious	102,674	563,444	460,770
Check (Multi-Bay)	Pg.F-117	8,262	71,419	CMDM	Serious	8,262	71,419	63,157
Check (NT)	Pg.-F-54	9,060	125,699	CMDM	Serious	9,060	125,699	116,639
Check (NT)	Pg.F-83	20,540	468,190	CMDM	Serious	20,540	468,190	447,650
Spillway (NT)	Pg.F-79	1,319	151,545	CMDM	Serious	1,319	151,545	150,226
						585,717	3,995,095	3,409,378

(1) CRIT applied HKM Replacement Cost

	Cost, $
HKM Structure Rehab Cost for Key Canals & Laterals (HKM total for all 23 1structures listed in Appendix D at D-1 to D-8.)	5,354,930
Remediation Cost Adj. for (CMDM, *serious* or *critical*) Key Canals and Laterals (Cost from "Difference" column above.)	3,409,378
Revised Remediation Cost (HKM total plus cost from "Difference" column above.)	8,764,308
Adjust for Appropriate Contingency Factor (HKM total plus "Difference" column above plus revised contingency factor.)	9,465,528

CRIT Table 3. Estimated Cost of Unaddressed Deficiencies

	Canal and Lateral O&M Roads				Canal Lining
	14-foot Wide Roads		16-foot Wide Roads		
	One Side	Both Sides	One Side	Both Sides	
Quantity, miles	138	276	138	276	64
Unit Cost, $/mile	65,050	65,050	74,342	74,342	2,161,483
Total Cost, $	8,976,845	17,953,690	10,259,251	20,518,502	138,334,912

PREPARED STATEMENT OF HON. VERNON S. FINLEY, TIBAL COUNCIL CHAIRMAN, CONFEDERATED SALISH AND KOOTENAI TRIBES OF THE FLATHEAD NATION

Dear Chairman Barrasso and Honorable Members of the Committee,

I respectfully request your review of this correspondence and ask that it be considered our testimony for the hearing record on S. 438, the IRRIGATE Act.

We greatly appreciate that Senators Barrasso, Tester, Daines, Hatch, Enzi and Bennett introduced S. 438. As one of the 16 Tribes with a BIA Irrigation project whose maintenance has been deferred far more than it should have, we are in agreement with the statements that the bill's sponsors have made both when introduced and at the recent hearing. Sadly this is just one more example of how the lack of funding to and from the BIA has resulted in various types of reservation infrastructures being allowed to deteriorate. Regardless of whether we are talking schools, roads, water systems or irrigation projects, the fact is that for decades our trustee has simply turned a blind eye, or at least an unrealistic one, to his responsibilities in this regard. It is unfortunate that lawsuits seem to be the only way to force our trustee to act on his fiduciary duties but in this case we are certainly appreciative that you recognize how important viable irrigation projects are to the economy of so many Indian reservations and even surrounding off-reservation communities. These projects affect thousands of both Indians and non-Indians who reside on or near those reservations. In order to resolve this infrastructure problem, both the authorizing and appropriations committee of the Congress are going to have to be realistic and admit that these programs simply cannot work without an infusion of new funds. Some of you may be familiar with the oft cited example of this which is that the Indian Health Service receives $3,348 on a per capita basis for providing health care to the Indian people whereas the US is spending $4,817 on a per capita basis for Federal Employee Health Benefits, $7,154 for health care services to Veterans and $11,018 per Medicaid beneficiary.[1] In the area of Forestry the BIA's budget allows for expenditures at $2.82 per acres where the US Forest Service spends $8.57 per acre.[2] Data for police, for schools and for infrastructure including irrigation and water all tell the same sad song of unconscionable spending

---

[1] "Fulfilling U.S. Treaty and Constitutional Obligations: Honoring Promises of Justice, Health and Prosperity." A report submitted to the US Congress by the Department of HHS, in conjunction with the FY 2013 Budget

[2] Report Number 3 of the congressionally established Indian Forest Management Assessment Team (IFMAT-III)

levels for Indian programs when compared to any other Federal beneficiary including those for whom there is *not* a fiduciary responsibility. We are encouraged that S. 438 (hopefully in an expanded version as discussed below) is an indication that Congress realizes that these types of inequities cannot be allowed to continue.

The Flathead Indian Irrigation Project (FIIP) dates back more than a century to 1908, when Congress authorized construction of the irrigation project using the Mission Mountains as a water source. It was built bay and is owned by the Bureau of Indian Affairs. FIIP includes an irrigation storage, distribution and delivery system serving about 127,500 irrigated acres on the Flathead Indian Reservation. This irrigation system includes 17 dams and reservoirs, approximately 1,300 miles of canals and laterals, and about 10,000 structures. Structures include fish protection facilities located where water is intercepted or diverted from streams and rivers. As is the case with other BIA irrigation projects, the BIA has deferred needed maintenance and the Operation and Maintenance (O&M) funds collected from water users simply do not generate enough money to overcome the backlog of deferred maintenance. O&M funds essentially pay for day to day operation. As a result, land that could be irrigated probably is not being irrigated and the water that is used is being used inefficiently. Furthermore, bull trout are a threatened species that live in the rivers and streams coming out of the Mission Mountains on our Reservation and the diversion of water for irrigation purposes increases the burden on this fishery. A more efficient irrigation project would benefit bull trout as would improvements in canal screening.

So there are economic, job creation and environmental reason why we support S. 438. And frankly, if you look at the amount of water that should have been protected for use on Indian reservations over the course of the last century that was instead diverted to off-reservation irrigation and water projects, it is about time that Indian reservation projects in Reclamation Act states were able to benefit from the Reclamation Fund! This is another reason to support the pending bill.

In the last Congress, Senator Baucus along with Indian Affairs Committee Members Tester, Hoeven, Johnson, Udall, Franken and Heitkamp, together with Senators Harkin, Heinrich, Klobuchar and Walsh introduced S. 715, the "Authorized Rural Water Projects Completion Act." Then-Congressman Daines introduced a House companion bill. The bill as introduced would have benefitted about seven rural water projects around the country, including two in Montana (Rocky Boy's/North Central Montana and Ft. Peck/Dry Prairie) that are not, under present circumstances, securing sufficient funding to complete their construction on a remotely timely basis.

When the bill was marked up the Senate Energy and Natural Resources two provisions were added to it that would benefit the Flathead Reservation. The first would have allowed the 16 BIA Irrigation Projects around the US to also access the new Treasury Department fund (the bill was proposing to create, accessing funds otherwise intended for the Reclamation Fund. A second amendment was adopted allowing this same new fund to help fund the costs of Indian Water Rights Settlements. The bill was then reported to the full Senate but was not taken up on the floor. We viewed the amended bill as being one that was sorely needed and an innovative approach to dealing with problems that have been longstanding. The Reclamation Fund is taking in far more each year than the Congress is spending on the Fund's authorized activities so this as a source of funding makes eminent sense to us.

We have spent well over a decade negotiating a water rights settlement with the State of Montana and the United States and that settlement package in now pending in the State Legislature, having just passed the State Senate. We are hopeful that it will pass after which it would, among other actions, need to be ratified by the US Congress. As has been the case in which tribes have settled their senior water rights against the US and their home states, the settlement would need federal funding to be implemented. Senate Report 113-167 accompanying S. 715 stated the situation well:

> *Settling Indian water rights claims rather than litigating them is generally seen as being advantageous for all parties and has been formal federal policy since the George H.W. Bush Administration (55 Fed. Reg. 9223 (1990)), so it is in the national interest to ensure a conducive atmosphere to settling water rights claim.*

> ***

> *Any agreement binding the United States as a party must be approved by Congress and most of the water settlements enacted from 1978 to present make funding for settlements contingent on the annual appropriations cycle. With funding for settlements uncertain, tribes and other parties have been increasingly concerned over whether projects authorized in water settlements legislation will be timely completed. Some tribes whose settlements were enacted nearly 20 years ago still must lobby for funding to keep projects on schedule every year. Such uncertainty makes it less and less likely tribes will continue to look toward settlements as a viable option which will lead to continued uncertainty over water rights in the arid west.*

For years the Congress has struggled to come up with a funding mechanism to pay the federal share of Indian water rights settlements. We recall that former Senator Pete Domenici (R-NM) introduced various proposals on how to accomplish this. One bill, S. 1186, was entitled the Fiscal Integrity of Indian Settlements Protection Act of 2001" and it addressed the manner by which Indian water settlement were scored and ensured that the BIA's budget be held harmless for the cost of the settlements. It allowed for up to $200 million in budget authority to be dedicated toward funding such settlements. In his introductory remarks Senator Domenici pointed out that negotiated Indian settlements provide more water to the tribes and are less expensive bill to the Federal government. Among its cosponsors were former Senators Allard and Kyl, certainly two members who took a back seat to no one in their concerns about federal deficits but who fully realized how essential it was to settle Indian water claims. I am attaching Senator Domenici's introductory comments that included a supportive statement from the Ad Hoc Group on Indian Water Rights. Members of that group included, among others, the Western States Water Council.

In 2012, the Senate Indian Affairs Committee held an oversight hearing entitled "INDIAN WATER RIGHTS: PROMOTING THE NEGOTIATION AND IMPLEMENTATION OF WATER SETTLEMENTS IN INDIAN COUNTRY." At that hearing then-Vice Chairman Barrasso very poignantly made the point I am trying to emphasize in this testimony when he said,

> "Water is a vital resource, as we know, in any community, including Indian communities. We all know that a community cannot thrive without an adequate, reliable supply of water. And yet many Indian reservations lack the basic water supply and water delivery systems that many of us living in non-Indian communities almost take for granted. Safe and adequate water supply facilities are lacking in approximately 12 percent of American Indian and Alaska Native homes. That compares to 1 percent of the homes for the general population of the United States. The lack of reliable, potable water supplies contributes to a wide range of health, social and economic problems on many Indian reservations."

Mr. Chairman, you hit the nail on the head when you spoke those words in 2012 and they are certainly still true today. To that end we believe the Indian water settlement and rural waters components contained in S. 715 from the previous Congress are integral to any legislation affecting water infrastructure on Indian reservations. We therefore urge you and the members of the Committee to add Title II and Title III from S. 715 back into S. 438 when you mark up the bill. The funding levels for those sections contained in S. 715 as reported should also be included.

Thank you for your consideration of the perspective of the Confederated Salish and Kootenai Tribes.

PREPARED STATEMENT OF THE CONFEDERATED TRIBES OF THE COLVILLE
RESERVATION

The Confederated Tribes of the Colville Reservation (''Colville Tribes'' or the ''CCT'') appreciates the Committee holding a hearing on S.438, the Irrigation Rehabilitation and Renovation for Indian Tribal Governments and Their Economies (''IRRIGATE'') Act. The CCT wishes to thank Chairman Barrasso and Vice-Chairman Tester for introducing this important legislation.

The CCT fully supports the IRRIGATE Act as a first step in providing Indian country with a path to completing long overdue irrigation infrastructure. Apart from the Indian irrigation projects that have already been authorized, the CCT would ultimately like to see a path forward for those tribes that are developing irrigation projects to address longstanding needs. The Colville Reservation falls into this category. The CCT offers this statement for the record to highlight some of the challenges that the CCT and its members continue to face in absence of any irrigation infrastructure.

The Colville Reservation was established by the Executive Order of July 2, 1872. At that time, the Colville Reservation consisted of all lands within the Washington Territory bounded by the Columbia and Okanogan Rivers, extending northward to the U.S.-Canadian border. As established by the 1872 Executive Order, the Colville Reservation encompassed approximately three million acres.

During the 1880s, the Colville Tribes came under increasing pressure to cede the ''North Half'' of the Colville Reservation, in large part because it was rich in minerals. A federal delegation was dispatched to the Reservation to seek a cession of the Tribes' lands. In 1891, many of the tribes residing on the Colville Reservation approved an agreement under which they ceded the North Half to the United States. The North Half is approximately 1.5 million acres and is bounded on the north by the U.S.-Canadian border, on the east by the Columbia River, on the west by the Okanogan River, and on the south is separated from the south half of the Colville Reservation by a line running parallel to the U.S.-Canadian border located approximately 35 miles south thereof. With the exception of the northern boundary, both the North Half and the present day reservation are surrounded by the waters of the Columbia and Okanogan Rivers.

It is ironic that the Federal Government has never constructed or provided any assistance for the CCT to establish an irrigation project on the Colville Reservation despite the presence of the Grand Coulee Dam on the Colville Reservation. The Grand Coulee Dam and its reservoir, Lake Roosevelt, supplies water to commercial farming interests in central Washington State. The area of central Washington where this farming occurs is referred to as the Columbia Basin. Congress established the Columbia Basin Project (CBP) to supply water to more than one million acres in this area. The Bureau of Reclamation (BOR) administers the CBP.

According to the BOR, the yearly value of the CBP is $630 million in irrigated crops, $950 million in power production, $20 million in flood damage prevention, and $50 million in recreation. The project itself involves costs that are difficult to determine. The farms that receive irrigation water must pay for it, but the payments account for only a small fraction of the total cost to the Federal Government. Some critics describe the CBP as an example of a federal subsidy to a relatively small group of farmers in a place where it would never be economically viable under other circumstances.

In contrast to the CBP, the CCT believes that given the opportunity to establish irrigation on the Colville Reservation, it could grow the economy not only of the CCT but of the surrounding non-Indian communities as well. The CCT has long been interested in developing an on-reservation irrigation project. The reasons for this include the following:

- The Federal Government made promises to the CCT in connection to the construction of the Grand Coulee Dam that the CCT would benefit from the irrigation opportunities the Dam would provide. Although some initial work was conducted, no irrigation infrastructure ever materialized.

- The tribes that compose the CCT irrigated lands for agricultural purposes prior to western contact in the Columbia Basin, which is known to our elders as Moses Gardens.

- The CCT manages instream water for beneficial public use such as salmon restoration efforts and utilizing irrigation infrastructure would reduce the competition between agriculture and salmon restoration efforts.

- The Okanogan River on the western reservation border is critically endangered by off reservation orchard irrigation in the spring and summer. Surface and ground water pumping deplete river water flows and increase the water temperatures. Salmon mortality increases every year. Supplemental irrigation water delivered to the head waters of the Okanogan River from the Columbia River would benefit tribal and non-tribal irrigators and salmon populations.

- Global warming and climate change has reduced annual precipitation. The CCT's semi-arid region depends on ground and surface water for domestic and irrigation needs. Our water wells are going dry. Currently there is a moratorium on any additional water services in the town of Nespelem, where the headquarters of the CCT is located. New irrigation infrastructure could replenish water supplies needed for growth.
- The U.S. Department of Agriculture, the Farm Service Agency, and the Natural Resources Conservation Service have programs to encourage tribal members with farming related business. The benefits these programs provide, which include grants and loans, are not accessible or feasible to tribes or tribal members without irrigation. Developing new irrigation projects on tribal lands would therefore allow tribal member farmers and ranchers the opportunity to participate in the agricultural economy as do non-Indian businesses on reservation lands.

The CCT again thanks Chairman Barrasso and Vice-Chairman Tester for their leadership on this issue. The future economic growth of the Colville Tribes depends on our ability to utilize the water that surrounds the Colville Reservation. We look forward to continuing to work with the Committee and assisting in moving the IRRIGATE Act forward in both the Senate and the House.

PREPARED STATEMENT OF TSOSIE LEWIS, CEO, NAVAJO AGRICULTURAL PRODUCTS INDUSTRY

Introduction

Good afternoon Chairman Barrasso, Vice Chairman Tester, and members of the Senate Committee on Indian Affairs. I am Tsosie Lewis and I am the Chief Executive Officer of the Navajo Agricultural Products Industry (NAPI), an agricultural enterprise chartered under the laws of the Navajo Nation (''Nation''). I am pleased to submit this prepared statement for the record relating to the Committee's legislative hearing on the Irrigation Rehabilitation and Renovation for Indian Tribal Governments and Their Economies Act (''IRRIGATE Act,'' S.438).

Background on the Navajo Indian Irrigation Project

In 1868, the United States Senate ratified a Treaty with the Nation which recognized the importance of agriculture to the self-sufficiency of the Navajo people.

In 1962, after years of intense negotiations between the Nation, the State of New Mexico, and the United States, Congress authorized the Navajo Indian Irrigation Project (''NIIP,'' Pub.L. 87483), to fulfill, in part, the United States' treaty obligations to supply water and a farming operation for the Nation.

The plain language of the 1962 Act, as well as its legislative history, makes clear the Federal obligation to build an 1 10,630-acre, irrigated-farm.

It was originally estimated that the NIIP would be completed in approximately fourteen years, in tandem with a companion project—the San Juan-Chama Project. The Nation made valuable concessions in exchange for the NIIP, allowing water from the San Juan Basin (to which the Nation had valid claims) to be transported to the Rio Grande Basin in New Mexico for the substantial benefit of non-Navajos.

The San Juan-Chama Project was completed in 1976, and the residents and businesses of the Rio Grande Basin have been enjoying the benefits of the bargain for nearly forty years while the NIIP, whose construction began in 1964, is only seventy-five percent complete.

The 1962 Act authorized $135 million to build the substantial physical infrastructure for the NIIP, and in 1970, Congress amended the Act to increase the authorized appropriations to $206 million.

In 2005, the Bureau of Indian Affairs (BIA) indexed this figure to 2005 dollars and estimated that there might be as much as $229 million in funding that could be appropriated without the need for a fresh authorization.

NAPI's Operations and Economic Importance

In April 1970, NAPI was established by the Navajo Nation Council as a tribal enterprise to manage and operate the NIIP. The idea behind NAPI was to manage the NIIP, create economic opportunities for the Navajo people and to build a foundation of commitment, pride, and dedication to their Nation.

Today, NAPI operates a 75,000-acre farm in Farmington, New Mexico, generating annual revenues of $223 million to the Nation and San Juan County. NAPI and its contractors employ more than 425 Navajo people in the Four Corners Area, and purchases tens of millions of dollars in goods and services both locally and across the Nation.

In its operations, NAPI has stressed the use of state-of-the-art technology and environmentallyfriendly practices. Its agribusiness features state-of-the-art farming equipment, including hightech radio control, and a computerized center-pivot irrigation system that reduces operational costs and efficiently manages water resources.

NAPI produces premier "Navajo Pride" brand agricultural products, including alfalfa, corn, feed, wheat and small grains, potatoes, and pinto beans. NAPI also operates a flour mill and leases land for cattle grazing, as well as for specialty crops.

Our products have earned the distinction of being "New Mexico Grown" by the New Mexico Department of Agriculture.

NAPI's operations are manifested in the international arena as well. In 2006, thanks in large measure to then-Congressman Tom Udall, a NAPI delegation travelled to Cuba and entered an executive trade agreement to sell to that country a variety of NAPI products.

While the Bureau of Reclamation, a contractor to the BIA, is responsible for the planning, design, and construction of the NIIP, the BIA has the sole responsibility, including funding requirements, to complete the NIIP.

Through its Operation & Maintenance Department, NAPI manages the operation and maintenance of the NIIP through a contract entered into pursuant to the Indian Self-Determination and Education Assistance Act. NAPI also manages Operations and Maintenance (O&M), On-Farm Development (OFD), and an Agricultural Testing Research Laboratory.

NIIP Funding Inadequacies

Annual funding for the NIIP construction was approximately $26 million per year during the Clinton Administration and $14 million during the Bush Administration. Beginning in fiscal year 2009, the annual budget request and consequent funding level for the NIIP has been a paltry $3 million. The fiscal year 2016 budget request proposes $3.4 million for the NIIP.

Despite the 1962 Act, federal funding to complete the final three 11,000 acre blocks of the NIIP is wholly inadequate. In addition to funds for new construction, the unavailability of O&M funding is resulting in the gradual deterioration of existing infrastructure by creating a large deferred maintenance backlog. As a result, NAPI and the Nation have been forced to work with the U.S. Department of the Interior and the Congress to re-program construction funding to the O&M account.

The BIA Irrigation O&M account nationally receives approximately $11 million annually and is used primarily for court-mandated payments, statutory requirements, and water storage costs. Currently, more than one-third of the $3.4 million NIIP O&M funding pays for electricity for pumping.

NAPI has made significant economic contributions despite the fact that the NIIP is only threequarters complete. An economic analysis recently issued by Compass Lexecon shows that the federal failure to complete the NIIP has cost the Nation billions of dollars in lost revenue and untold economic opportunities that will not return.

The Irrigation Rehabilitation and Renovation for Indian Tribal Governments and Their Economies Act (S. 438)

On February 10, 2015, Chairman Barrasso (R–WY) introduced the IRRIGATE Act (S. 438), establishing an Indian Irrigation Fund in the Treasury of the United States.

The bill directs the Treasury Secretary to transfer $35 million annually into the Indian Irrigation Fund from the existing Reclamation Fund through fiscal year 2026. These funds are to "carry out maintenance, repair, and replacement activities" on Indian irrigation projects and gives priority to Indian irrigation projects that have not been funded for the last fifteen years.

In addition, S. 438 directs the Interior Secretary to consult with tribal governments and conduct a study that evaluates options for improving programmatic, project management, and performance of irrigation projects managed and operated by the BIA.

We believe the NIIP might satisfy the eligibility criteria provided in S.438. Should broader legislation be considered similar to the "Authorized Rural Water Projects Act" (S. 715) introduced by then-Sen. Max Baucus, we also believe the NIIP would be eligible for the funding authorized in that legislation.

In the meantime, NAPI strongly supports S.438 and urges the Committee to expedite consideration of the bill in the weeks ahead. Further, we wish to thank Chairman Barrasso and Vice Chairman Tester for their leadership on this important matter.

Conclusion

The history of federal funding and support of the NIIP and related activities reveals that partial and delayed funding has resulted and continues to result in delayed or derailed economic opportunities, job creation, and chronic problems in maintaining physical infrastructure and irrigation equipment.

Thank you for providing me the opportunity to submit this statement for the record, and I stand ready to assist the Committee in any way I can.

———

PREPARED STATEMENT OF THE CHIPPEWA CREE TRIBE OF THE ROCKY BOY'S RESERVATION

While the Chippewa Cree Tribe is appreciative of Chairman Barrasso's initiative in introducing this legislation, we are concerned and perhaps a little mystified about what happened to the provision authorizing funds for the completion of the authorized rural water projects from S. 715. The language in S. 438 started off as an amendment that Senator Barrasso offered last year to a larger bill known as the the "Authorized Rural Water Projects Completion Act" (S. 715). That legislation was originally introduced by Senator Baucus and 10 other Senators. Now it would appear that the basic underlying component of S. 715 for rural water projects has disappeared and all that is left is a bill for irrigation projects. While we commend Senator Barrasso for supporting Indian irrigation projects, we are at a loss to understand how the main reason for S. 715 is gone and one of the two amendments is all that is left. We urge the Senate Indian Affairs to put the language for rural water projects back into S. 438.

As introduced by Senator Baucus and ten other Senators, with a companion bill in the House introduced by then Congressman Daines, S.715 would have authorized the creation of an account in the Treasury Department accessing funds otherwise intended for the Reclamation Fund so that a number of pending rural water projects, both on and off-Indian reservations in Iowa, South Dakota, Minnesota, Montana, South and North Dakota and New Mexico could be completed. As the Committee Report (113-167) accompanying the bill indicated, over one million Americans have no drinking water piped into their homes and over 2.4 million Americans have critical drinking water needs. The report also points out that the unmet need for potable water supplies in the 17 western States exceeds $5 billion and exceeds $1.2 billion for specific water supply projects on Indian reservations.

Honorable Committee Members, there will never be economic development and job creation on these lands, and the health disparities that so negatively impact many Indian people will never be addressed unless we have this most basic of infrastructure -- clean and reliable drinking water. These projects including the Rocky Boys/North Central Montana Rural Water Project have been funded on an annual basis in such small amounts that they are literally not keeping up with inflation and at least seven, including ours, are experiencing a significant backlog. By stretching funding out unnecessarily over an additional three decades and building at a snail's pace due to lack of sufficient funding, the Committee report indicates that the additional costs could be as high as $1 billion nationally. Please look at the attached chart that shows the impact of funding this project at the present pace. Not only does it take forever to be completed (if at all) but look at the waste of $200 million in the taxpayer's money under the present funding scheme. Think about the suffering on our reservation and among our neighbors that goes along with this delay.

It is important to note, as the Committee Report did, that the Reclamation Fund has been running a surplus of $960 million a year each year since 2005 and that the Rural Water provision found in S. 715 authorized the delivery of Reclamation Fund dollars in the amount of $80 million annually through the year 2035, CBO stated that pay-as-you-go procedures do not apply to this legislation because it would not affect direct spending or revenues.

Please also consider our history on this project. In 1997, the Chippewa Cree Tribe of the Rocky Boy's Reservation, the State of Montana and the United States negotiated a settlement of the Tribe's water rights claims. A compact ratifying this agreement was approved that year by the Montana Legislature and signed into law at the Federal level by President Clinton in December of 1999 as PL 106-163, the "Chippewa Cree Tribe of the Rocky Boy's Reservation Indian Reserved Water Rights Settlement Act." Among its other components, the law provided a water allocation of 10,000 acre feet of water to the Tribe from Lake Elwell, which is also known as Tiber Reservoir, a facility that is owned and operated by the Bureau of Reclamation. Tiber is 50 miles from the Rocky Boy's Reservation.

On December 12, 2002, President Bush signed S.2017, the Rocky Boy's/North Central Montana Regional Water System (RBNCMRWS or "Rocky Boys/North Central Water Project") Act of 2002 (PL 107-331) as the final step in the federal approval process of transporting that water to the reservation and the beginning of a project to improve the quality of life for the Tribe and residents of north central Montana. In addition to providing a water supply for the Tribe, the project included the provision of water service to residents of Chouteau, Hill, Liberty, Pondera, Teton, Glacier and Toole counties in Montana.

While we appreciate the funds we have received to date for the Rocky Boys/North Central Water Project there is a large population of Indian and non-Indian people in Montana who are physically and financially dependent on the completion of this project and the provision of water promised in these two federal laws. At this point -- 18 years after the enactment of law settling the Tribes' water rights and 13 year after the enactment of a law providing for the construction of water delivery systems serving the Reservation and thousands of Montanans in surrounding communities — we have received less than one-quarter of funds needed to complete the construction of this rural water project. Please be aware that the nature of the existing water in this part of Montana is such that the Department of Environmental Quality has implemented a number of boil water orders for our local communities. Many reservation residents suffer from H. pylori, a serious water borne infection in the stomach.

Please add the rural water provisions back into S. 438 during the legislative consideration of this bill.

Thank you.

PREPARED STATEMENT OF HON. CLEMENT J. FROST, CHAIRMAN, SOUTHERN UTE INDIAN TRIBE

Chairman Barrasso, Vice-Chairman Tester and members of the Committee, thank you for your attention to Indian irrigation projects and for holding the above-referenced hearing.

On behalf of the Southern Ute Indian Tribe ("Tribe") and the Southern Ute Indian Tribal Council, I am pleased to submit this prepared statement for the record and to register the Tribe's strong support for S 438, the Irrigation Rehabilitation and Renovation for Indian Tribal Governments and Their Economies (IRRIGATE) Act. The Southern Ute Indian Tribe has a long-standing and continuing interest in working with Congress to address the problems of failing irrigation infrastructure in Indian Country. The Tribe remains greatly interested in stopping and reversing the decades-long deterioration of Indian irrigation projects and firmly believes that the passage of S.438 would be an important first step in doing so.

The Tribe is heartened that the Congress continues to deliberate the best method for the United States to meet its obligation to work with tribes to resolve an issue of great importance for many tribes. Our Tribe has a particular interest in this legislation because the Pine River Indian Irrigation Project (PRIIP) on the Southern Ute Indian Reservation has suffered many decades of neglect and mismanagement by the Bureau of Indian Affairs (BIA). These years of ignoring the needs of the PRIIP and its users, both Indian (85 percent of the project's land base) and non-Indian (15 percent) residents of the Reservation, have resulted in a rehabilitation and maintenance backlog estimated at up to $60 million.

The PRIIP has been an important part of the economy and culture of the local community since the late 1800s. Its continued deterioration through the decades has caused economic hardship for all of its users, both tribal members and non-Indians.

The project long ago reached a point where conditions created a disincentive for aggressively practicing agriculture. Now, as the Tribe pursues greater efforts to maintain a diversified economy, the state of the PRIIP continues to be a major impediment to economic progress.

In spite of intermittent efforts by the BIA, the disrepair of the PRIIP system has still not been adequately evaluated and catalogued. Nonetheless, previous analysis shows the increasingly dilapidated state of the project:

- only an estimated 15 percent of the project's 175 miles of canals can be considered in good condition;
- some of the project's major diversion structures date to the 1930s and have had no major rehabilitation or improvements since the 1960s;
- an estimated 40 percent of the project's irrigable acreage is not being irrigated, and a significant amount of that simply cannot be irrigated given the current state of the project;
- the project's largest canal, serving over 4,500 acres of Indian and non-Indian land, has breached and experienced multiple major bank slope failures in less than a year and its ability to deliver a full supply of water in the coming season is questionable;
- dozens of smaller drop structures constructed pre-1920s have collapsed and simply been abandoned, exacerbating erosion of the system;
- many structures have failed due to erosion, poor design, and poor maintenance;
- ditches have been abandoned and lands that were previously irrigated have become derelict, requiring costly rehabilitation; and
- erosion has created miles of incised canals and ditches where elevated headgates no longer allow for the diversion of water to lands that historically were irrigated.

The amount of work necessary to bring the system to a minimal level of adequate functionality is staggering.

The Tribe has committed to fixing the PRIIP, and has previously worked with this Committee on various legislative efforts specific to the PRIIP; but, at this time, we firmly believe the broader tribal approach to planning and funding concepts outlined in S.438 are the best vehicle for finally getting attention and resources paid to the PRIIP.

We recognize that we are far from the only tribe facing these issues and, therefore, we strongly support a broad solution that addresses the greater problem across Indian Country. Furthermore, we believe that the solution to the problem of irrigation project rehabilitation, maintenance, and continued operation must include sound planning intended to create long-term agricultural sustainability and economic viability. Such an approach must be built on an effective partnership between the federal government and the tribes, and S. 438, by requiring adequate study, pre-planning, and, most importantly, consultation with tribes and irrigation system users, would ensure such a partnership is developed before repair work begins.

Importantly, the IRRIGATE Act would also authorize tribes to assume responsibility for repair projects through Indian Self-Determination and Education Assistance Act contracts and compacts. Last, while we understand that passage of S. 438 would result in large costs to the federal government, those costs are spread out over a number of years and, unfortunately, given the many decades of the federal government's failure to properly maintain Indian irrigation projects, a significant federal price tag is simply unavoidable. Unlike other areas of federal largesse, however, the funds authorized by S. 438 would finally serve those for whom the federal government stands as trustee and, in many cases, carry through on solemn treaty promises made to tribes by the Federal Government over a century ago.

Thank you for considering these comments and including them in the record. If the Tribe can be of assistance to the Committee as it considers this legislation, please do not hesitate to contact me. Last, we urge the Committee to favorably report S. 438 and seek swift passage by the full Senate.

PREPARED STATEMENT OF THE NAVAJO HOUSING AUTHORITY (NHA)

The Navajo Housing Authority (NHA) is thankful for this opportunity to submit testimony to the United States Senate Committee on Indian Affairs for the legislative hearing on, ''S. 710, the Reauthorization of the Native American Housing Assistance and Self-Determination Act of 2015 (NAHASDA).'' We appreciate the Committee's efforts to highlight the importance of Indian housing, and to hold a hearing to examine the provisions of S. 710. We thank Chairman John Barrasso for introducing this bill and we look forward to working with him on its passage.

The NHA hopes that the Committee will find this testimony both informative in understanding our views on the NAHASDA reauthorization, and to understand and appreciate the direction that NHA is headed in building sustainable and vibrant communities.

Background on NHA and the Navajo Housing Need

Completed in August 2011, the NHA's housing needs assessment study established a baseline housing need on the Navajo Nation of 34,100 new homes and another 34,300 existing homes are in need of major repair—which equates to approximately $9 billion. After holding a series of regional workshops and consultations with all 110 Navajo communities the total housing need was re-adjusted to 50,445 new homes.

It was evident that to meet this overwhelmingly unmet housing need NHA must break with the status quo and employ new strategies towards an integrated and comprehensive approach that maximizes our funding, facilitates large-scale housing development while investing and building sustainable communities. Furthermore, in 2012, the NHA developed a five-year expenditure plan (2013–2017) that set aggressive spending goals to bring down the large balance of undisbursed Indian Housing Block Grant (IHBG) funds. The organization has been successful in meeting its targeted goals, and to-date has spent approximately $329 million, built 580 new housing units, modernized 964 older housing units, and funded the development of 16 group homes and acquisition of 3 housing units for persons with disabilities since implementing the expenditure plan on October 1, 2012. Moreover, we have broken ground for the Bluestone Development—our first sustainable master-planned community that will provide an additional 165 housing units.

It is important to note that NHA is more than just a construction agency that builds new homes. On a day-to-day basis we cover an array of housing services that includes the management and operation of over 9,200 housing units including 29 office facilities and oversight of an additional 2,000 units operated by other local housing providers. NHA is also addressing longstanding deferred maintenance of older housing units built before NAHASDA that require modernization and retrofits to meet Section 504 accessibility requirements for both dwelling and non-dwelling facilities. Beyond housing, NHA engages in crime prevention and safety activities as well as model projects that include, but are not limited to: Boys & Girls Club and other youth facilities, women and children shelters, college student housing, elderly care homes, supportive housing, and other relevant projects.

NHA Views on S. 710

NAHASDA was created in the spirit of self-determination to provide tribes local control and decisionmaking of affordable housing programs for their tribal communities. We appreciate the advances in S. 710 that enhance local decisionmaking authority and recognize that tribes have the sovereign authority to set standards and guidelines within their tribal community. More specifically, we support the following changes included in S. 710:

1) Clarifications relating to program and non-program income;
2) Use of tribal prevailing wage and a single environmental review for projects funded by multiple federal agencies;
3) Ability for tribes to set maximum rents and homebuyer payments;
4) Technical correction on maximum leasehold terms to reflect those included in the Helping Expedite and Advance Responsible Tribal Homeownership Act (HEARTH);
5) Open the eligibility of TDHEs to apply for the ICDBG program; and
6) Expansion of the Public Assisted Housing Drug Elimination Act of 1990 to include clean up due to methamphetamine damage.

We feel these changes will help streamline the ability of NHA to effectively manage and operate its housing programs and services.

Native American Veterans Supportive Housing

Veterans housing and supportive services is a major need on the Navajo Nation. The 2011 housing survey conducted of 11,500 households on the Navajo Nation showed that those homes housed 31,213 families. Of those, 2,726 were households that included at least one veteran. As noted earlier, many of these homes, nearly 30,000 existing homes, are in need of major repair. However, because there is no other housing available, often the veteran and their family are forced to live in dilapidated housing that could easily be consider substandard or inhabitable.

NHA was pleased that Congress authorized HUD to set aside funds for the Native American VASH program through the 2015 "Cromnibus" bill. NHA is anxious to be a part of the Native American VASH Program. However, as we expressed in our comments to HUD, this program can only be successful if the design fits with the current NAHASDA programs and services. Our main request is that the Native American VASH program ultimately employ a true tribal-federal partnership to ensure the program will meet the needs of the target population. This would mean that the Veterans Administration (VA) would need to consider sub-contracting with tribal housing programs and other tribal departments those additional supportive services for Native veterans. Delivery of supportive services to a large population with remote geographic locations like the Navajo Nation may create challenges for VA personnel to provide timely and comprehensive supportive services.

Tenant-based rental assistance versus project-based rental assistance. The biggest problem with using the tenant based rental assistance vouchers on the Navajo Nation is the lack of private or non-profit housing for renters. Therefore, the Native American VASH language should allow rental assistance to be used on housing currently included in the housing stock of the tribal housing programs. If vouchers could be used on current NHA rental properties, then we can set aside a fair number of units for potential VASH renters and build more rental units for other families. Currently, NHA relies on using our rental vouchers for only Section 8 approved properties off the reservation. This solution will not help veterans who wish to stay on the reservation close to a family who is helping to support their recovery.

As for project based assistance, NHA is ready today to use the project based rental assistance. Our sustainable community master plan project will create several integrated communities that will include public rental, homeownership coupled with economic development opportunities. These master-planned communities will be financed and leveraged with federal products and programs, and the project based assistance can be an element that would work into the development of the master-planned communities. NHA's timeline for this project is moving fast, and to be of greatest value the project based assistance would need to be available within the next year.

Demonstration Program for Alternative Privatization Authority

A new demonstration program is being proposed as Title IX of NAHASDA. The new program would allow tribes and TDHEs to work with investor partners to provide for the housing needs of the tribe. There should be an option for tribes or TDHEs to participate with some of their funding allocation while maintaining their participation in the regular NAHASDA program with the remainder of their block grant funds.

Effect of Undisbursed Block Grant Amounts

Recently, the Navajo Nation Council passed legislation number CF–7–15, that expresses the position on NAHASDA reauthorization. In brief, the position states that the Navajo Nation supports NAHASDA reauthorization, however the Nation expresses opposition to any "withholding" language that does not have an effective date of 2018.

We appreciate Chairman Barrasso for hearing NHA's and the Navajo Nation's concerns, and including in S. 710 an effective date of Jan. 1, 2018 for any "withholding" language. NHA would like to note that we have consistently upheld to our commitment to address our undisbursed funds. In fact, we have spent a total of $329 million to date since the start of our expenditure plan in 2012 and we currently have an 80 percent expenditure rate—these numbers show both a significant decline in unspent IHBG funds and a significant increase in spending IHBG funds. Our aggressive five year expenditure plan that started on October 1, 2012 will spend down the backlog of undisbursed funds by the end of FY 2017. The effective date in S. 710 is in-line with our targeted expenditures goals—NHA will have brought down our balance of undisbursed IHBG funds before the "withholding" language takes effect.

The Committee should be assured that NHA is not carelessly spending this money, we have a prudent development strategy to ensure that our expenditures are making strategic investments into our Navajo communities. We must note that it takes nearly three to five years just to build homes on the Navajo reservation. There is considerable planning involved just to make housing development a reality.

Conclusion

NHA was one of the first Indian Housing Authorities to be established, and it was the Navajo Nation leadership who gathered with other tribal leaders in 1996 to advance NAHASDA's initial passage. We were honored to work with a broad coalition of tribes and Congress to pass this important piece of legislation. We hope that Congress will work to swiftly pass a reauthorization bill that recognizes and honors the spirit of self-determination and self-governance. NHA must be clear that we cannot support a bill that does not include a 2018 effective date for any "withholding" language for undisbursed IHBG funds—Congress should recognize that NHA has gone above and beyond to prove to Congress that we are meeting our spending goals and we respectfully ask that our request is honored.

NHA appreciates the opportunity to provide you this written testimony for the record, and we would be please to answer any questions that the Committee or the Senate may have.

————

PREPARED STATEMENT OF THE UTE INDIAN TRIBE OF THE UINTAH AND OURAY
RESERVATION

Chairman Barrasso, Vice Chairman Tester, and Members of the Committee on Indian Affairs, including Mr. Hatch, Mr. Enzi, and Mr. Daines, sponsors of the bill, thank you for the opportunity to testify on S. 438, the "Indian Tribal Energy Development and Self-Determination Act Amendments of 2011." The Ute Indian Tribe is a federally recognized Indian tribe and the beneficial owner of the Uintah Indian Irrigation Project, which is held in trust by the United States Secretary of the Interior. The Uintah Indian Irrigation Project is one of the 16 irrigation projects managed by the Bureau of Indian Affairs. The Tribe supports S. 438, and requests that the bill include the amendments described in the final section of our testimony.

Historical Background of the Ute Indian Tribe of the Uintah and Ouray Reservation

The Ute Indian Tribe is made up of three Bands, the Uintah, White River, and Uncompaghre Bands. The Tribe was organized pursuant to the provisions of the Indian Reorganization Act of June 18, 1934 (48 Stat. 984, as amended). The Tribe's Uintah and Ouray Reservation (Reservation) is located in northwestern Utah.

The Federal Government's allotment policies resulted in substantial losses of the Tribe's Reservation lands. The Reservation originally included approximately 4.5 million acres. The Tribe now owns about 1 million acres of trust lands.

The Uintah Indian Irrigation Project

Utah is the second most arid State in the country. It rains little in the summer and, therefore, the only source of water is the winter snow melt and the ability to store it. Water management has long been recognized early and often by the Federal Government as a necessary component of the development of the Tribe's lands, including allotments, in the settlement of the Reservation. For example, in his annual report for 1905, the Commissioner of Indian Affairs observed of the Ute Indians:

> The future of these Indians depends upon a successful irrigation scheme, for without water their lands are valueless, and starvation or extermination will be their fate. The circumstances are such that delay or hesitation will be fatal because all rights to waters in Utah are based on the priority of use.

Thus, on June 21, 1906, the United States Congress authorized the construction of irrigation systems to irrigate "the allotted lands of the Uncompahgre, Uintah, and White River Utes in Utah," with "the cost of said entire work to be reimbursed from the proceeds of the sale of the lands within the former Uintah Reservation." Now known as the Uintah Indian Irrigation Project, the Congressional authorization provided:

> That such irrigation systems shall be constructed and completed and held and operated, and water therefor appropriated under the laws of the State of Utah, and *the title thereto until otherwise provided by law shall be in the Secretary of the Interior in trust for the Indians,* and he may sue and be sued in matters relating thereto[.] (34 Stat. 325, 375–76) (emphasis added).

Under this authority, the Bureau of Indian Affairs (BIA) constructed a system to irrigate 78,950 acres of allotted land, via an extensive system of canals and ditches to convey water from three river drainages: the Strawberry-Duchesne, Lake Fork-Yellowstone, and the Uinta-Whiterocks rivers.

Also, in anticipation of the project, the United States, through the BIA, made application to the Utah State Engineer in 1905 to appropriate water from the State of Utah for the Uintah Indian Irrigation Project (prior to the establishment of the *Winters* Doctrine in 1908 of federallyreserved Indian water rights). Some ten to fifteen years later, the State issued water right certificates for the lands under the

Uintah Indian Irrigation Project to the United States, which now holds the water rights in trust for the Tribe, allottees, and their successors.

A program was initiated to level, clear, plow, and fence the Indian allotments to get them into cultivation. Tribal funds were used for this purpose. By 1908, over $330,000 had been spent on the irrigation project; although less than $7,000 had been paid to Indian laborers, and, out of the 78,950 acres within the irrigation project, about 25,000 acres had already been sold to non-tribal members. In 1916, of 37,380 Indian allotted acres, 13,134 acres were irrigated. Construction ended in 1922, but no water storage facility was included in the project.

In 1916, the United States initiated litigation in federal district court to protect the Ute Tribe's water rights because of increasing conflicts between the Ute water users of the Uintah Indian Irrigation Project and their non-Indian neighbors over the water allocations in the Lake Fork, Yellowstone, Uinta, and Whiterocks Rivers. *United States v. Cedarview Irrigation Company et al.*, No. 4427 (D. Utah 1923), and *United States v. Dry Gulch Irrigation Company et al.*, No. 4418 (D. Utah 1923). The Federal District Court determined the quantity and priority of Tribal water rights under the Uintah Indian Irrigation Project on the Uinta-Whiterocks River Basin and the Lake Fork-Yellowstone River Basin.

The court issued two federal decrees recognizing the Ute Indian Tribe's *Winters* reserved water rights as present-perfected water rights in those two Basins with an 1861 priority date, the date of the creation of the Uintah Valley reservation (re-characterizing the water rights originally filed by the Indian Irrigation Service with the State of Utah prior to the 1908 *Winters* decision). The two Federal Court Decrees provided 179,315.07 acre-feet per year for irrigation of 59,771.69 acres of Tribal allotments within the Project, with a total irrigation diversion limit of 3 acre-feet per year per acre, and permitted year-round diversion of water for domestic, culinary, and stock watering uses. Project lands irrigated by the Duchesne River consist of approximately 18,000 acres.

BIA has responsibility for the management of the Uintah Indian Irrigation Project. There have been a century of reports studying the problems of the Uintah Indian Irrigation Project. All of them conclude that the continuous deferred maintenance of the project and failure to construct the required storage facilities that would support irrigation through the mid-to-late summer months has significantly impacted the ability of the Ute Indians to efficiently farm there.

In some of the more recent reports, HKM Associates, a tribal contractor, issued a report in 1982 and found from a survey of 3,425 Uintah Indian Irrigation Project irrigation structures showed that 84 percent were in need of repair or replacement. Then, in 1988, both the Tribal engineer and the Department of Interior concluded that $75 million was needed to repair and rehabilitate the Project.

In an attempt to address these problems, under the 1992 CUPCA, the Secretary retained trust responsibilities to the Ute Tribe and allottees of the Project, but turned over the daily operation, maintenance, rehabilitation, and construction of the Uintah Indian Irrigation Project to a water users' organization. Under the 1992 CUPCA, the Secretary is required to "use funds received from assessments, carriage agreements, leases, and all other additional sources . . . for the Uintah Indian Irrigation Project administration, operation, maintenance, rehabilitation, and construction . . . " Section 203(f), CUPCA.

However, Congress has not provided any funds to the Uintah Indian Irrigation Project for these activities—even though over half of the landowners under the Project are Indians, who continue to struggle with their ability to pay a sufficient level of assessments that could support the on-going costs of long-time deferred repair, replacement, maintenance, and construction of the Project works and desperately required storage facilities.

Another report issued by BIA in 2008 asserted: "The Uintah Irrigation Project has deferred maintenance needs in excess of $86.1 million to bring the aging, deteriorated infrastructure up to current standards. The majority of our diversion structures lack any safety features to keep personnel safe while operating gates and cleaning debris for the upstream side of the structures. There is no fencing or gates to prevent the general public from getting on any of our structures of features."[1]

Finally, a General Accounting Office (GAO) report issued in 2006 on the Indian Irrigation Projects[2] stated that the BIA estimated the cost for deferred maintenance

---

[1] *See* U.S. Dept. of Interior, BIA, Western Region, "Operation and Maintenance Guidelines: Uintah Indian Irrigation Project, Uintah and Ouray Agency" (Dec. 23, 2008).

[2] GAO Report to the Chairman, Subcommittee on Interior and Related Agencies, Committee on Appropriations, U.S. Senate, "Indian Irrigation Projects: Numerous Issues Need to be Addressed to Improve Project Management and Financial Sustainability," GAO–060–314 (February 2006).

at its 16 irrigation projects, including the Uintah Indian Irrigation Project, at about $850 million for 2005. And the BIA, Office of Trust Services, Division of Water and Power, issued a Program Review of the Uintah Indian Irrigation Project in 2011 and found many deficiencies in the BIA Agency's management and administration of the Project, resulting in resource mismanagement that adversely affecting the Project water users.

Despite Congressional direction, the Tribe has yet to see the comprehensive rehabilitation of the Project or the construction of storage facilities necessary for the operation of the Project. The Ute Tribe's and allottees' treatment by the Federal Government with regard to funding for the Uintah Indian Irrigation Project has been particularly egregious when one important fact, unique to the Ute Indians (and maybe only one other Indian irrigation project) is considered: the United States is designated by statute as the trustee of the Uintah Indian Irrigation Project, where the Secretary of Interior holds the Project in trust for the Indians. Act of June 21, 1906, 34 Stat. 325, 375–76.

The Need for Tribal Storage

The need for tribal storage for the Uintah Indian Irrigation Project has been clearly and repeatedly documented for over 100 years, since the early 20th Century. Indeed, it is well known that irrigation cannot be successful in an arid environment without storage. An extensive historical record supports the conclusion that the Federal government, through both BIA and the Bureau of Reclamation, has long recognized the fact that both natural flows and storage are needed to make farming under the Project successful.

The following excerpts briefly highlight the Federal Government's acknowledged awareness of its obligation to manage the Project through storage facilities:

U.S. Indian Service (1916):[3] The ditch-riders "were powerless to overcome the diversion of all the water from Lake Forks and Uintah rivers above the headgates of the ditches of this project diverting from the lower reaches of these streams."

BIA (1938):[4] "[T]he Indian Service has not constructed storage reservoirs, although storage water would be a valuable asset."

BOR (1965): "This [Uintah Indian Irrigation] project is substantially completed with the exception of storage requirements."

BOR (1968):[5] "Storage regulation for irrigation such as that which would be provided by the Uintah Unit . . . is urgently needed."

BOR (1975):[6] "There is an urgent need for storage facilities to regulate the streamflows to match the irrigation demand pattern."

DOI (1977):[7] "The Secretary of the Interior has fiduciary responsibility for the welfare of the Ute Indian Tribe. The Tribe has supported the Bonneville Unit to assure an orderly development of water resources for the Tribe through the Central Utah Project. Water for the Bonneville Unit is available through agreements made by the United States and the Ute Indian Tribe."

BIA (1978):[8] "Water storage has never been provided [to the Uintah Indian Irrigation Project]. . . and is greatly needed."

BOR (1978):[9] "Substantial areas of potentially irrigable Indian lands are entirely without a water supply. . . ."

BOR (1980):[10] "No storage reservoirs were built [for the Uintah Indian Irrigation Project], and therefore only a partial supply could be furnished."

In Title II of CUPCA, Congress provided funds for the Central Utah Water Conservancy District (District) to develop alternative, smaller storage facilities for the Uintah and Upalco Units, which would serve the Tribe's Uintah Indian Irrigation Project. Unfortunately, as planning commenced the Tribe soon found they were yet

---

[3] Correspondence from the Dept. of Interior Engineer to H.W. Dietz, Superintendent of Irrigation, dated January 20, 1916, regarding problems with the Uintah Irrigation Project.

[4] U.S. Bureau of Indian Affairs. *A Study of Economic Conditions on the Uintah Irrigation Project, Utah. Including Recommendations for the Adjustment of Irrigation Assessments with Suggestions for Project Composition, Rehabilitation and Administration.* September, 1938.

[5] U.S. Bureau of Reclamation. *Uintah Unit, Central Utah Project, Feasibility Report.* May, 1968.

[6] U.S. Bureau of Reclamation. *Uintah Unit, Central Utah Project, Report for Certification of Physical, Economic, and Financial Feasibility.* April, 1975.

[7] U.S. Dept. of Interior, Water Projects Review Office, Preliminary Information and Data Sheets for Bonneville Unit (Bureau of Reclamation, March 15, 1977).

[8] U.S. Bureau of Indian Affairs. *Statement of Position Water Resource Issues Uintah and Ouray Reservation.* June, 1978.

[9] U.S. Bureau of Reclamation. *Uintah Unit, Central Utah Project, Definite Plan Report.* August, 1978.

[10] U.S. Bureau of Reclamation. *Uintah Unit, Central Utah Project, Status Report.* June, 1980.

again not benefitting. The Tribal allocation for storage in the proposed projects was smaller than contemplated under the original Upalco and Uintah Units, and would not fulfill the storage needs of the Tribe under the Uintah Indian Irrigation Project. By the late 1990s, it became clear that the projects as designed were not in the best interest of the Tribe. In 1999, the Tribe decided against supporting the replacement projects as planned. Although the Tribe withdrew support for these particular reservoirs, the Tribe did not give up on its pursuit for storage, nor was the obligation of the Federal Government to provide storage relieved.

Less than 9 percent of the irrigation water promised to the Tribe was ultimately developed. Compared to the total amount of water developed in the Uinta Basin by the CUP, less than 5 percent is directly made available to the Tribe.

Because of these shortages, the Tribe has sought to develop viable, environmentally sound storage facility options that will regulate the flows of Reservation streams and provide an ample and dependable water supply for the Tribe under the Project. Storage, combined with natural flow, is the only way the Tribe can fully develop its Reservation lands under the Project and put its reserved water rights to use.

Proposed Amendments for S. 438, the IRRIGATE Act

The Uintah Indian Irrigation Project is in a debilitated state and represents a significant hazard to individuals working for the Project and distributing the irrigation water and to those irrigating under the Project. To ensure that that the IRRIGATE Act fully addresses the Federal government's trust responsibility for the Tribe's Uintah Indian Irrigation Project and focuses funding on the most pressing issues for creating successful Indian irrigation projects, the Tribe requests that the following amendments, shown in underline, be included in the bill.

SEC. 201 REPAIR, REPLACEMENT, AND MAINTENANCE OF CERTAIN INDIAN IRRIGATION PROJECTS.

(a) IN GENERAL.—The Secretary shall establish a program to address the deferred maintenance needs of Indian irrigation projects, including the construction of storage needs, that—

    (1) Create risks to public or employee safety or natural or cultural resources; and

    (2) Unduly impede the management and efficiency of the Indian irrigation program.

SEC. 202 ELIGIBLE PROJECTS.

The projects eligible for funding under section 201(b) are the Indian irrigation projects in the western United States that, on the date of enactment of this Act—

    (1) are owned by the Federal Government, as listed in the Federal inventory required by Executive Order 13327 (40 U.S.C. 121 note; relating to Federal real property asset management); or

    (2) are held by the Secretary in trust for the Indians pursuant to Congressional authorization of the project; and

    (3) are managed by the Bureau of Indian Affairs (including projects managed under contracts or compacts pursuant to the Indian Self-Determination and Education Assistance Act (25 U.S.C. §450 et seq. or any other statute authorizing any such contract); and

    (4) have deferred maintenance documented by the Bureau of Indian Affairs.

SEC. 203 REQUIREMENTS AND CONDITIONS.

    (1) programmatic goals to carry out this title that—

        (A) would enable the completion of repairing, replacing, improving, , or performing maintenance on projects as expeditiously as possible;

        (B) would provide storage facilities to enable the projects to becomes feasible and profitable by having an adequate water supply;

    (2) funding prioritization criteria to serve as a methodology for distributing funds under this title, that take into account—

        (C) the extent to which deferred maintenance, or failure to provide storage, poses a threat to the ability of the Bureau of Indian Affairs to carry out the mission of the Bureau of Indian Affairs in operating the project;

        (D) the extent to which repairing, replacing, improving, or performing maintenance on, or the construction of, a facility or structure will—

            (iv) assist in protecting natural or cultural resources; and

(v) use modern irrigation technologies for the conveyance and distribution of irrigation water that will improve the efficiency of water management and use by a project.

SEC. 206. ALLOCATION AMONG PROJECTS.

(b) PRIORITY.—In allocating amounts under section 201(b), in addition to considering the funding priorities described in section 203, the Secretary shall give priority to eligible Indian irrigation projects serving more than 1 Indian tribe within an Indian reservation or required by Congress in the authorizing project language to be held by the Secretary in trust for the Indians, and to projects for which funding has not been made available during the 15-year period ending on the day before the date of enactment of this Act under any other Act of Congress that expressly identifies the Indian irrigation project or the Indian reservation of the project to address the deferred maintenance, repair, or replacement needs and/or storage needs of the Indian irrigation project.

LETTER FROM HON. JIM ALLEN, REPRESENTATIVE, HOUSE DISTRICT 33, FREMONT COUNTY AND THE WIND RIVER INDIAN RESERVATION

Dear Senator Barrasso,

Thank for sponsoring the IRRIGATE Act. I write today in support of this important bill. It will, if passed, provide much needed rehabilitation funding for our dilapidated and crumbling irrigation delivery canals, ditches and structures on the Wind River Indian Reservation of Wyoming. This reservation is home to two tribes, the Eastern Shoshone, Northern Arapaho and several non-tribal residents totaling approximately 17,000–20,000 people. It is important to note that the decay of the irrigation system on this reservation is due to a backlog of uncompleted federal maintenance and to shortfalls in Congressional funding. This bill will go a long way in bringing this aging and decadent system back up to the former standards. By repairing the system, precious water will be better utilized, crops will improve, our local economy will improve and water will be saved for downstream users. Just as importantly, water will be delivered fairly and equitably. Everybody wins.

However, I would caution Congress to designate these irrigation rehab funds to be spent on repairing the broken irrigation system, not hiring more BIA adminstrators or funding more studies. That has already been done and Billings BIA Irrigation staff, the Tribal Water Engineer, both Tribal Councils and irrigators know exactly what needs fixed and where. This money could be put to good use immediately if this bill passes.

I represent a large portion of the reservation and most of its irrigated lands in the Wyoming House of Representatives. I am also on the House Agriculture, Public lands and Water committee and the state of Wyoming knows well the ancient status of reservation irrigation infrastructure and the need for funding. The state does not have enough money to adequately fund repairs, but more importantly, the Federal Government has a trust responsibility to the tribes and it has fallen decades behind in funding irrigation repairs on the reservation. We need this bill.

One last point. Since there are also non-tribal landowner/irrigators residing on the reservation, it is imperative they are counted and heard too in policy development regarding prioritizing irrigation rehabilitation projects and timelines. Water is appurtenant to the land regardless of tribal membership status.

Thank you for bringing this very important and beneficial bill. I hope it passes.

LETTER FROM FRED TAMMANY, CHAIRMAN, RAY CANAL WATER USERS ASSOCIATION

Dear Senator Barrasso,

I am writing in response to your proposed legislation, the "IRRIGATE" Act for rehabilitation of the deteriorating irrigation systems on Indian Reservations throughout the West. Our water-user's group, the Ray Canal Water Users Association, is comprised of two hundred seventy-eight (278) members and manages 10,260 acres on the Wind River Indian Reservation, home to both the Shoshone and Northern Arapaho Tribes.

As you are aware from your visit with us last summer that was hosted by the Tribal Water Engineers Office, our system is close to collapse and in desperate need of rehabilitation after years of neglect by the controlling BIA. Your legislation would work to correct these inadequacies would benefit all users of the Wind River Irrigation Project and fulfill the trust responsibilities of the United States.

The Ray Canal Water Users Association and the Crowheart Water Users Group on the Wind River Reservation have demonstrated that prudent maintenance, volunteers, and lower overhead costs make considerable improvements to the fair and equitable delivery of water to the irrigators. With the help of this legislation, our groups would be able to capitalize on best-use practices that have developed over the years and make a more efficient system that would end up benefiting all occupants of the reservation.

In closing, our Ray Canal Water Users Association looks forward to the passage of this legislation and rolling up our sleeves with a "Get 'er done" spirit so that we can all reap the rewards from this act. Our only concern is that the funds need to be correctly allocated in order to avoid creating more unnecessary administrative positions and to avoid paying for studies that have already been completed. There have been many studies completed regarding the irrigation situation on our reservation, but no action has been taken until now. As water users, we are quite familiar with the inadequacies of the system and the areas of critical importance in the rehab project; our experience should be capitalized upon and could be invaluable to the successful economic basis of this project. We also hope that there will not be liens or debts assigned to the users as a result of this Act. Agriculture has and hopefully always will be an important contributor to the gross national product and the world with a little help from our friends in Washington D.C.

This legislation is a last line of hope if our irrigation system is to survive. We cannot thank you enough for the concern you have demonstrated for our plight, for work towards the opportunity to improve our system, and for your contributions to agricultural communities, Fremont County, the State of Wyoming, and the United States of America.

———

LETTER FROM THE CROWHEART BENCH WATER USER'S ASSOCIATION (CBWUA) AND THE "A" CANAL WATER USER'S ASSOCIATION (ACWUA)

Indian Affairs Committee,

The Crowheart Bench Water User's Association (CBWUA) and the "A" Canal Water User's Association (ACWUA) would like to express our support for the "Irrigation Rehabilitation and Renovation for Indian Tribal Governments and Their Economies Act" or the "IRRIGATE ACT"

The CBWUA and ACWUA are irrigator managed irrigation systems in the Crowheart Unit of the Wind River Reservation. These organizations manage their systems, totaling approximately 10,500 acres, through a Cooperative Assistance Agreement (CAA) with the Bureau of Indian Affairs, directed by an elected board of irrigators. Since the inception of these organizations, many positive steps have been taken to improve the delivery and overall operation of the BIA irrigation systems in the Crowheart area. Dilapidated structures have been replaced, miles of canals and laterals have been cleaned, and multiple individual farm turnouts have been updated. All of these tasks have been completed while maintaining irrigation operations and maintenance assessments that are significantly lower than those paid by other units that fall under BIA management on the Wind River Unit. Cost savings on administration, (board members are on a volunteer basis), low overhead (the associations do not own equipment or employ operators, but instead hire contractors) and donated labor by irrigators have made this arrangement feasible. However, like all the systems on the Wind River Unit, the deferred maintenance needs we have inherited are significant. We have been benefited in recent years from funding provided through legislation spearheaded by the late Craig Thomas and others that was administered by the Tribal Water Engineer's office and matched by funds provided by the Wyoming Water Development Commission. These funds have served to rehabilitate many structures on the Wind River Reservation, inc luding two major diversion structures in the Crowheart area. Unfortunately, the 7 million dollar amount provided by the Wyoming Water Development Commission and the Thomas legislation is far from adequate to address the rehabilitation needs of the irrigation infrastructure on the Wind River Reservation.

The "IRRIGATE ACT" would provide much needed funding to help cover the costs of rehabilitation, enhance safety features, and modernize the systems in Crowheart and throughout the reservation. In our experience managing our systems, dollars go much further when they are put to work on the ground, not to add unnecessary administrative positions or purchase very expensive and often inefficient equipment and operators. Our systems have been studied extensively, most recently in 2006. Studies are a valuable tool to ensure proper allocation of funds within a project, however those landowners who pay the operations and maintenance assessments and have invested their time and efforts in improving their systems as we have in Crowheart should be considered authorities on their systems and should not be ignored. As irrigators, we would much rather see funds go to work on the ground than on yet another study. It is also critical that funds are not provided with strings attached, such as liens against the land serviced by the systems or debts that are assigned by those who do not own the land.

In summary, we are encouraged by the opportunities this proposed legislation will bring to the communities throughout the Wind River Reservation. The water is tied to the land in these communities and delivery of this water in an efficient manner is the key to the success of the operations in the area. Wateruser groups like those in Crowheart are critical to improving operations because those involved have a financial interest in their success. Thank you for your efforts on this legislation, and we look forward to working with the Committee in the future.